# Praise for
# CLOSE AND GROW RICH

*"Once again John Palumbo has captured the essence of success in his latest book Close and Grow Rich. From the first couple of chapters where John talks about "Rewiring Yourself" on through this book to the section on "Reasonable Doubt"...., John provides a "Garmin-Style" Roadmap for the salesperson that wants to become a better closer and grow rich now! You will not be able to put this book down!!"*

**JACK GALLAGHER**, MIRM, President, GMG Incorporated

*"Find out what business you are REALLY in! John has identified 14 skills you can put to use immediately to dramatically improve your ability to close and increase your income exponentially."*

**CAROL FLAMMER**, Managing Partner, mRELEVANCE.com

*"A brilliant follow up to What's your Sales DNA? John delivers 220 Volts of high impact insight that infuses your preexisting skill set with a new state of mind. A positive charge that inspires immediate action."*

**RAY BOULÉY,** MIRM, President, Next Step...the origin of ideas

# CLOSE
## AND GROW
# RICH

# CLOSE
## AND GROW
# RI¢H

**Fourteen Untapped Skills You Already
Have To Close Your Next Deal**

## JOHN A. PALUMBO

For general information on our other products and services, please call (904) 448-1100.

ISBN: 978-1-934381-01-4

John@JohnPalumbo.com
www.CloseandGrowRich.com
www.JohnPalumbo.co

# DEDICATION

To my Aunt Rosalie and Uncle Tony.

*"I've heard it all, John, and my numbers are still down! What can you possibly tell me about closing that will actually help me close more deals? What are the skills I've overlooked? What exactly am I missing?"*

*What if I told you that you're not missing anything? That you already have everything you need?*

## ACKNOWLEDGMENTS

One's thoughts and achievements are shaped by those around us, and I have been fortunate to have been surrounded by some of some of the greats in the industry. It would be impossible to mention everyone who contributed; however, there are some individuals who deserve special mention. That list includes Bonnie Alfriend, Tom Richey, Bob Schultz, S. Robert August, Bill Webb, Roger Fiehn, Meredith Oliver, Melinda Brody, Jack Gallagher, Roland Nairnsey, and Myers Barnes. I should also mention Zig Ziglar, Brian Tracy, Mark Victor Hansen, Tony Robbins, and Dr. Denis Waitley, to name a few, for their endless inspiration and wisdom.

This book really wouldn't have made it to press without the help of a few key players. Thanks to my editor, Brandon Toropov, and Jerry Dorris for their ability to materialize even my wildest thoughts. And Yvonne Fort, Linda Rossell, and Maggie Rogers, my incredibly indispensible team. My gratitude also goes out to Mike Friday, Gene Lambert, Ed Randle ,Tim French, and Chuck D'Accardi, who have stood by me through the many years – you are true friends.

Many authors thank their family, and I'm sure most readers probably think it's merely an obligatory thanks. The truth is families offer support, encouragement, insight, confidence, and so much more. Thanks, especially, to my father, Leonard, Aunt Rosalie and Uncle Tony, Heidi, and my daughter, Morgan.

# Table of Contents

## Part I: Beyond the Black Belt

## Part II – The Fourteen Skills

# Part III – Epilogue

# Overview

## The Art of Not Asking
## for the Check

'm not the first to say it, and I certainly won't be the last: If you can't close, you can't sell.

If you sell for a living, your close may happen in any number of ways. If you're a salesperson, closing is your job. Maybe your kind of close has to happen after a presentation in a conference room, over the phone, on a shop floor, in a showroom, in an individual consumer's home, in a boardroom, during a "walkthrough," a guided tour, or during a demonstration of something your organization created. One thing is certain, though – whenever and wherever your close is supposed to happen, *you and you alone will be responsible for it.*

Now, many salespeople don't get this. They actually say things like: "I'm good at everything else in the process ... I just don't close very well. I'm fine with meeting new prospects and giving presentations, and I'm comfortable with taking incoming orders. The only thing I'm not comfortable with is closing people who aren't yet ready to buy. I just don't want to pressure people."

Ask yourself these two questions:

*Question One: If I am only good at meetings and conversations that never turn into business, am I really a "salesperson"?* (Personally, I think "company spokesperson" or "professional tour guide" would be more accurate.)

*And Question Two: If all I do is take down specifications from people who have already decided to buy, is that "selling"?* (Not in my world. That's a whole different discipline, called "customer service.")

If you sell for a living, closing is your responsibility. Period.

## "Yeah – but how?"

That's a question I get all the time. People say, "John, you say it's my responsibility to close the deal. All right. It is my responsibility. I'm already trying everything I know. What else can you give me that I haven't heard? I bet that, over the years, I've gotten all the advice there is to get about closing sales, and you know what? Anything that seemed promising, I'd already tried! I've heard it all, John, and my numbers are still down! What new twist is there that will actually help me close more deals?

What exactly am I missing?"

What if I told you that you already have everything you need?

What if I told you that you already know how to close more business and grow rich? What if I told you that your job is simply to awaken skills you have right now? What if I told you there were skills that you've forgotten, overlooked, or (is it possible?) never even knew you had in the first place?

What if I told you that you simply haven't implemented untapped interpersonal skills waiting inside you as you read these words – skills that come from the source Napoleon Hill, author of the landmark book *Think and Grow Rich*, identified as INFINITE INTELLIGENCE?

What if I told you there was an untapped Sales Master within you, waiting patiently to help you put those skills to use?

Would you listen?

Or would you say …

## "High-pressure sales tactics don't work for me!"

I hear this, too. "In my (industry/market/world/department/ zip code), high-pressure tactics always backfire. Not sometimes, mind you, but always. Who wants to be pushy?"

What if I told you that high-pressure is not what this book is about?

What if I told you that it's about changing the direction of the pressure you're used to seeing salespeople apply?

What if I told you that pressure is good … that it's necessary to close any deal … but that most salespeople usually apply pressure foolishly, from the outside?

What if I told you that, if you implement what I'm about to share with you, you would never want to, or need to, use high-pressure tactics with any of your prospects?

What if I told you that this book would show you how to use skills you already possess … skills you can awaken through an inner power that's always with you?

What if I told you that, right now, you could create the kind of subtle *internal* pressure that gets prospects to tell *you* that it's time to get started?

I call this process "The Art of Not Asking for the Check." And it is a matter of taking control of your mind. Just as Napoleon Hill demonstrated that attracting wealth is primarily a mental process, I have learned, after closing well over a billion dollars' worth of deals, that attracting closed business is a mental process. *In fact, it's precisely the same mental process.*

But it takes a little practice, and, because people are complicated entities with a whole lot of moving parts, there is no one single reliable strategy for getting that process going with any given prospect. There are, by my count, fourteen basic strategies, each connected to a given skill, for getting that buying process going, and they all interconnect with one another. What we're talking about, really, is a mental art: the art of using one or more of those fourteen skills at the right time, and with the right outcome.

What if I told you that you could learn that mental art more quickly than you ever imagined?

This book gives you fourteen interconnected lessons in reawakening the closing skills you already have – skills that make it easier for people to tell you that they want to move forward and buy from you. If you're not closing enough business now, that's because you've allowed these skills to become dormant. I'd like to show you how to wake them up. Once you do, you will have mastered the art of selling … and you will be ready to *Close and Grow Rich.*

I'd like to teach you that art. Will you let me?

If so, turn the page.

# PART ONE

Beyond the Black Belt

# CHAPTER ONE

## The Closing Fundamentals

Think of me as your closing coach.

My job is to help you focus on the steps that will get you into the "closing zone" – pay-dirt, if you will. Your job is to practice and execute as I suggest. Yes, I will challenge you.

Now, coaches in all disciplines are big on reinforcing the fundamentals with the people they're coaching. And that's true in our case as well. For each and every one of the fourteen "closing skills" we're going to

**I'm going to challenge you.**

reawaken, there is one *fundamental,* underlying idea that supports you. If you master this idea, you will know which skill to use, and with whom, in any given situation, in the flash of an instant.

Let me put it more plainly. If you locate and grasp this one simple principle, then this book will work for you. If you don't, then this book probably won't work for you. As you ponder that, let me tell you plainly that the principle has been mentioned within these pages several dozen times.

Somewhere, as you read, the single, simple idea I'm talking about will leap from the page and present itself to you with great audacity and confidence ... if you are ready for it. When this happens, you will know without any hesitation that you have come across the "secret." When you grasp it, grab a great, big, colorful marker, go to your calendar, and circle the day you made the discovery. That day will mark the critical turning point in your selling career.

At this point, I want to follow in Napoleon Hill's (large) footsteps and offer a brief suggestion that may provide you with a clue by which the secret can be recognized when you finally come across it. It is this: *Achievement and financial success may seem like external realities, but they are really nothing more or less than the IMAGES of the destination you select with the "mental compass" you hold within your mind at all times.*

If you're ready to master the fourteen "closing skills" that are really only ONE skill, you already possess one half of the secret. (The other half has to do with desire.) I am confident you will take action on the secret the moment it comes your way.

# CHAPTER TWO

## "Black Belt" and Beyond

A note of guidance is in order here. The first ten "unawakened" closing skills we will be discussing in this book are what you will need to get to "black belt" status as a closer – but did you know that there are different degrees among the real-life martial arts masters who attain the coveted black belt?

It's true. If you're a student of, say, tae kwon do, you will go through a number of colored belt

**Good ... or great?**

levels before you attain the black belt – and even then, you won't be finished. As a new black belt, you will aspire to move from first-degree black belt to second, from second-degree black belt to third, and so on.

So I'd like you to consider the "final four" of the fourteen "unawakened" skills in this book to be your personal long-term project. Mastering them will take time, effort, and personal commitment from your side ... but did you pick up this book to become a *good* closer, or did you do so in order to become a *great* closer

# CHAPTER THREE

## Magnetizing Your Mind

The human mind is "magnetized" in a certain direction by the thoughts that we ourselves allow to flourish inside it. If we consciously choose to harbor thoughts that inspire passion and confidence and belief in what we ourselves do, and if we cultivate those thoughts until they occur authentically and automatically, then we find that our mind points in a certain direction … a direction that literally generates commitments from other people, as a power plant generates electricity. And commitments from other people are what closing is all about.

Note: This book is not about "improving your attitude" or "thinking positive," at least not in the sense that most salespeople understand these concepts: as a passing parade, as a moment of passion during a meeting, as a fleeting resolution that comes and goes every January. I am talking about *rewiring yourself* so as to *habitually* eradicate the negative thinking that has, whether you realize it or not, been the actual cause of each and every obstacle to closing that has come your way.

# CHAPTER FOUR

## The People Business

You and I are salespeople. That means we're in the people business. Some people sell software and believe they're in the software business. Other people sell equipment and make the mistake of believing they're in the equipment business. And some people sell advertising and fall into the trap of believing they're in the advertising business.

So let's get clear on one thing. Whatever it is that you sell – let's call it "widgets" – you are not in the widget business. You are in the people business. And that means that, at the end of the day, you are in the "state of mind" business.

Salespeople who don't yet know that they're in the "state of mind"

> **Your state of mind is what you're "selling."**

business are, inevitably, poor closers. And poor closers, as the saying goes, raise skinny kids!

If we're in sales, and we don't want our kids to be skinny, it's incumbent on us to know, and to remind ourselves constantly, of what business we are really in. It's not hand holding. Not presenting. Not calling back week after week and leaving a message. It's closing. That's what we do for a living if we're salespeople.

Now, to get good at closing, we have to accept that our goal is, first and foremost, to affect the other person's state of mind. That's what every marketing book, every sales book, and every book on of the art of persuasion will tell you. But those books usually leave something very important out: It is literally impossible for us to affect another person's state of mind if we don't first take responsibility for *our own* state of mind.

> **You can't close effectively if you have no control over your own state of mind.**

Contrary to popular belief, closing is not about manipulation. It's not about sneaky maneuvers. It's not about intimidation. It's about commitment to a certain state of mind.

The person who is most committed to his or her state of mind will be the one who affects the other person's state of mind. You cannot be an effective closer if you have no control over your own state of mind. And you cannot have control over your own state of mind if you do not have a passionate, burning *desire*. I'm talking about a special kind of desire: the desire not merely to *envision* your definite chief aim in life, but to *experience* it right now, as if it were already accomplished. Are you ready to reap the rewards for doing that?

Our mission is to cultivate a certain desire-driven state of mind – and only that state of mind – and then to become so committed to it that we routinely affect the mindsets of everyone we encounter … including our prospects.

Now – what, exactly, stands in the way of our doing that?

# CHAPTER FIVE

## What Stands in the Way?

To answer that question, I have to give you a little background on the "design" of this book. It's part of a two-book series. This book can be read alone, or in combination with its companion volume, *What's Your Sales DNA?*

For the next few pages, I'm going to operate on the twin assumptions that a) you really are willing to commit yourself to the goal of taking full control of your mental state and b) you have not yet read *What's Your Sales DNA?* (Of course, if you *have* read this book's companion volume, what follows will serve as a powerful "refresher course" and update on some of the key concepts there).

**How do Master Closers think?**

There are, in the world of sales, some salespeople who have

harnessed the power of their own minds. You've met them. We've all met them. These are people who project a certain powerful commitment to a burning desire the instant they walk into a room or pick up the phone – they are, to use the common term, "Master Closers." The odd thing is, these "Master Closers" aren't using the pushy, borderline-desperate techniques we see and hear so often in the media's portrayals of salespeople who are trying to "close the deal." They're on a whole different level. I call these people Sales Masters.

Surely *you've* had exposure at some point in your career to a Sales Master – to someone who achieved at a level that left you wondering, "What is he or she doing that I'm not?"

Unfortunately, that's the wrong question. We should be less concerned with copying the external things that the Sales Master does ... and more concerned with learning the internal management processes, the way the Sales Master thinks. The Sales Master manages his or her self-image, emo-

**Downloading the right "software."** tions, and experiences in a way that delivers a certain state of belief, a powerful, confident state of mind rooted in a burning *desire*. This state of mind becomes a matter of habit, something automatic that affects everyone with whom the Sales Master interacts.

Now, *why* does the Sales Master do that automatically?

I'll tell you why. The Sales Master has downloaded, and learned to operate, internal mental "software" that consistently *delivers* that confident state of mind.

So asking what this person "does" – externally – is really a waste of our time. We can't get the results of a Sales Master simply by dialing the phone the same number of times he or she does, or dressing in the same kinds of clothes, or saying the same things when we shake someone's hand. We have to figure out what this person does internally – how the Sales Master *thinks*.

# CHAPTER SIX

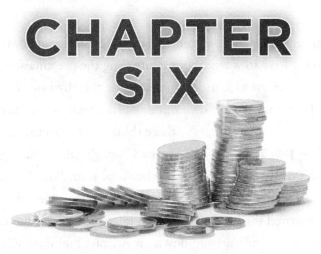

## The Sales Masters'
## Internal World

If, beginning today, you started managing your self-image, emotions and experiences ... thinking ... and experiencing your world the way top income producers do ... would your commission income go up or down?

You already know the answer. Your income would go up. *Why* would it go up? Well, I'll tell you why. For one reason and one reason alone: because you would be doing a better job of controlling your own state of mind. That means you would be projecting more confidence, thinking more creatively, and delivering more effective solutions to the people you would encounter during your selling day.

Think of what follows in this book as "software" for your selling career. If you learn to operate this software properly, you really can control your own mind – and that's the most important thing of all for any salesperson to control. If you control your own mind, you don't have to worry about controlling the presentation, or the dynamics of the face-to-face meeting, or the rhythm of the cold call. If you control your own mind, you *automatically* control all of those things ... and so much more.

**The parable of the earth mover.**

Earl Nightingale, in his legendary motivational recording *The Strangest Secret*, once told a story about this. He compared the human mind to a huge piece of equipment that he saw once while driving down an Arizona highway. What captured Nightingale's attention was an earth mover, capable of moving tons of dirt from one spot to another. The example I like to give for this earth mover sounds like this: Imagine the biggest monster truck you've ever seen – on steroids. It was just a tremendous piece of machinery, lumbering purposefully, straight down the highway.

What Nightingale noticed was that this massive piece of engineering was controlled, up at the very top, by a single small man with his hands astride an even smaller steering wheel.

With this story, Nightingale reminds us that the human mind is like that massive, powerful machine. Its potential is absolutely awe-inspiring. Its direction depends on the tiniest twist of our mental "steering wheel." We really are in control of the huge vehicle – if we choose to be. Let me follow Nightingale's lead and ask a question about that massive vehicle: What are our intentions as we drive it?

Do we aim to take control of the vehicle and guide it down the highway toward a destination of our choice? Or do we aim to take our hands off the steering wheel and allow the huge wheels to drift wherever they wish? Do we watch passively as the great vehicle careens into the gutter?

# CHAPTER SEVEN

## Close like the Masters

**B**y following the simple advice in this book, you're going to learn to close like a Sales Master does — by taking control of exactly the same machinery the Sales Masters use: the human mind. You're going to take the same steps as the "big dawgs." You're going to talk like they talk, and walk like they walk. Most importantly, though, you're going to think like they think.

Some people think effective closing is "done with smoke and mirrors." Nothing could be further from the truth! As the following pages will demonstrate, closing like a Sales Master is really a repeatable process ... a process that draws on talents you already have.

Skeptical? Don't be.

# CHAPTER EIGHT

## About This Book

T his book is broken up into small text chunks. I know your day is hectic and it's hard to come by long stretches of time for reading books. My goal has been to make it easy for you to finish off a chapter and get back here with me to start a new one the next time you have a few minutes to spend.

And that's exactly what I want you to do—as long as you see dividends coming back to you on your investment of time and attention. Your job will be to keep returning to these pages … if and only if you keep encountering ideas that you can use to improve your earning power as a salesperson. *And my job is to keep you coming back for more, chapter after chapter. Turn the page right now!*

# PART TWO

## The Close and Grow Rich Skills

## Finding Mastery

### Principle #1: We can only sell to the level at which we see ourselves.

*"Act the way you'd like to be and soon you'll be the way you act."*

– George W. Crane, nineteenth-century publisher, author, and motivational essayist

There are a lot of nicknames for people who take jobs as salespeople but who don't actually close sales. One of those nicknames is PTG. That stands for Professional Tour Guide. This is used in a variety of industries, including the housing industry. These are the folks who drive people around and tell a lot of stories … but never seem to get the prospect's pen moving across the paper. Nobody *sets out* to be a Professional Tour Guide. You become one by *refusing* to appeal to the Sales Master within yourself.

Early on in my career, and long before I realized I had mastered the first closing skill on this list, I made a fateful decision: *I am a Sales Master, not a tour guide.* You're going to have to make exactly the same decision. You're going to have to choose to embrace Mastery, and to see yourself as a Master in what you do.

## The decision

One decision makes everything else possible. One decision supports a burning *desire* to focus consistently on your definite chief aim in life. One decision makes it possible to experience that goal as a tangible *mental* reality before you experience it as a tangible *physical* reality.

Once you make your own fateful decision, you're going to find that you're taking exactly the same steps as the "big dawgs." You're going to find that you're talking like they're talking, walking like they're walking, and, most important of all, thinking like they're thinking.

*But the decision to see yourself as a Sales Master has to come first.* After all, closing sales is not a matter of tricking people into doing something they don't want to do. Pretending you can do that is absurd, unethical, and a recipe for career disaster. Closing deals consistently, at a high level, is more a matter of putting *yourself* on notice

**How do you see yourself?**

that you are committed to undertake all of what follows in your life as a Sales Master.

## The challenge

I am talking about seeing yourself as deserving success … and I am talking about taking personal responsibility for every aspect of your life, whether seemingly positive or seemingly negative.

Here's another way of putting that challenge: We can only sell to the level we actually see ourselves occupying. If we want to sell to top-level people, we ourselves have to assume top-level responsibility. If we want to sell at the top level, we have to see ourselves as worthy of *occupying* that top level.

At heart, we must believe we *deserve* to attain a certain specific level of success; in fact, we must believe that so powerfully that, internally, we see, feel, and hear ourselves as already having attained it. In other words, we *are* the top sales agent in our company, before we even post the numbers that confirm this for other people.

*If we want great things to "happen to us,"* then we have to take personal responsibility for literally *everything* that "happens to us." I put that phrase in quotes, because the idea that external events "happen" to change our world is a very limiting, and ultimately inadequate, way to look at the world. *We create our world.* At some level, we are responsible for it all.

If, today, you're not yet earning what you want to be earning, not yet closing at the level you want to be closing, not yet achieving what you want to be achieving, the answer to *why* that is can be found by consulting the nearest mirror. It should be clear to you from what I'm saying that, if you choose to *Close and Grow Rich*, you may need to make some changes in the way you envision *your relationship to the world.*

Right now, you may believe that external forces, events outside of your control, determine whether you can close effectively. That, in a word, is denial. And if you're in it right now, *you need to get out,* as in before you turn this page. *No, really. Before you proceed with another syllable of this book.*

**You will need to get out of denial mode for any of this to work. You and you alone are in control of what happens in your world. You are choosing, right now, whether or not to accept this responsibility before you continue reading.**

## "Good morning, Mr. President."

Here's a reality check for you. *You are the President. You* are the one in charge here. Right now, even as you read these words, you're sitting in your own personal Oval Office. On your desk is a sheet of paper. Written on that sheet of paper is a critical question: *How do you see yourself, and who do you consider to be responsible for the outcomes in your life?*

I'm here to remind you that *you and you alone* have the power, and the responsibility, to answer that question in a way that transforms your life. Not just today. Not just tomorrow. Forever.

## Margaritaville

I can also tell you that the answer to this "mother of all questions" *can easily be found* in many, many places – sometimes in places where you would least expect it. For instance, if you're listening carefully enough, you'll find the answer in the singer Jimmy Buffett's most famous pop song, "Margaritaville." To paraphrase Buffett in a way I feel he'd be certain to approve of: "Some people claim that there's a 'bad market' … or an 'economic downturn' … or a 'tough client' to blame for the way my life is now – but *I know it's my own damn fault.*"

## News flash!

We can only truly *lead* our lives – that is, go in the direction we want to go in life – if we acknowledge that we, ourselves, are the leaders of the expedition. We can only receive the rewards we want by accepting that we really are responsible for *everything* that happens, not only in our accounts and in our sales visits, but in our careers and our larger lives.

We are responsible for creating our own world and for placing ourselves at the very top of it. Nothing else of interest will happen until that happens.

There's an old saying that "no thought lives in the mind rent-free." You really do pick your thoughts. And that means you really do control your outcomes.

## The driver's seat

I've known many salespeople who were intimidated by people who had a lot of money. These salespeople felt like the rich were smarter or had greater insight on the world than they did. The truth is, the affluent are simply more confident in their business dealings than most people. *The money does not create the confidence – the confidence creates the money.*

The people you want to sell to *expect* to deal with someone with the same level of confidence that they have. Period. Why on earth would they buy from someone who is *less* confident than they are?

If they don't see that confidence, prospects will hit the "ejector seat" button when you try to sit next to them in the sales "car." If they do see that confidence, prospects will ask you to do the driving. It's that simple.

When you are dealing with your prospects, they expect you to have all the answers and be the problem solver. They expect you to be confident and bring solutions to the table so that they can make comfortable, quick decisions. Contrary to popular belief, price resistance is really not that big a factor (especially when you're dealing with affluent buyers) – *if* you are totally committed to what you are doing and *if* you are seen as the definitive informational resource.

Time really is money. If you are perceived as a person who knows *exactly* what is happening, as a person who can save both time and money, you will be in the sales "driver's seat" – and you will **close the deal.**

What are you going to do now?

No matter what has happened in the past, no matter how badly things have misfired, no matter how many times you may have watched opportunity slip through your fingers, the question you must face is a direct one, Mr. or Ms. President: *What are you going to do ... right now?*

Right now, at this second, there is someone within you who is indeed a breed apart ... someone who is willing to perform at a truly superhuman level, if only *you* are willing to *demand* that this Sales Master step forward. But making that demand requires a certain special kind of effort.

## The failure

Let me tell you a true story about a thirty-eight-year-old man who was, by all rational measures, a confirmed failure in life. When I say, "failure," I mean washed up. Repeatedly.

From his boyhood, he had the aim of being a world-famous concert pianist. He practiced relentlessly, morning after morning, in the predawn hours. As a young man, though, he failed at that goal of his. He simply didn't have the musical talent to put that career across.

He then got a job with a newspaper, and his family had high hopes for him in that field, too. But that position ended up going nowhere.

He then tried his hand at another goal: he would become a top-tier banking executive. He resolved to work his way up through the ranks to accomplish that aim, and got a job as a clerk.

He worked like a man possessed. But that career path didn't pan out, either.

Then he spent eight backbreaking years devoted to a brand new goal – the goal of building up a successful farming enterprise. He worked himself to the point of physical exhaustion, day after day. But his efforts were for naught. The farm went bust.

After that experience, he went into the military, but found he couldn't make a go of it. Before long, he opted to return to civilian life.

Next, he vowed to strike it rich by drilling for oil, and after some significant effort, he convinced his sweetheart to invest in his latest venture. After pushing that goal to what must have seemed to most thinking people to be the outermost limit, and after seeing no return whatsoever, he walked away from his stake and started looking around for a new career.

Within a few months, he received a rude surprise from that trickster Fate. He learned the very land he had been drilling on for oil had produced a millionaire's strike – for someone else. He lamented that he seemed to have a great skill for calling "heads" when the coin just tossed was about to come up "tails."

Next, he decided to try his hand at the world of retail. He opened up a clothing shop with one of his old Army buddies. Unfortunately, there was an economic downturn, and his market collapsed. The business went down in ruins.

At that point, he was thirty-eight years old, with no shop, no job, and no prospects. He had huge debts. Nothing, but nothing, that he had tried to do to produce wealth in his life had worked. And the entire world, it seemed, was against him.

If he had wanted to, this determined, hard-working man could have seen the world as a hostile and dangerous place, and could have been forgiven for seeing himself as someone who had been victimized by it, or who had, at least, been unable to control it. Clearly, he was a failure. But it was at this very point – at exactly this dark and dispiriting milepost in his life's journey – that this failure, an utterly defeated Kansas City haberdasher by the name of Harry Truman, opted to choose a different mental "path." He redefined himself.

He started work as a salesman. Yes, Harry Truman was a com-missioned salesperson – for the Kansas City Automobile Club. He found, to his surprise, he was pretty good at selling. He sold a thousand memberships. He wrote the following fateful sentence to his sweetheart, a conclusion with earth-shaking implications for anyone who cares to transform his or her own life:

**"If I want to be great, I have to win the victory over myself through self-discipline."**

*Harry Truman had found a new way to communicate with him-self, about himself.* That's how he found the Master within himself. By changing what he said to himself and by changing what he focused on.

Look at it again. Not only did Truman learn an important lesson about selling during this period, *he learned an important lesson about himself.* He himself was responsible for victory – nothing on the outside. He mastered that lesson. He sold a lot of memberships to the Kansas City Automobile Club. And along the way, he found he was pretty good at communicating with people.

What skills are waiting inside of *you* for *you* to awaken?

Please understand the real point of this story. At what had to have been the darkest point of his economic life, Harry Truman *found someone else within his own head, someone he could rely on.* He found a Harry Truman who was "a breed apart." He found Mastery. It was Mastery that allowed him to support his family *as a commissioned salesperson* while he pursued, on the side, what had become his new passion and what eventually became his calling – politics.

Now, then. What was the external result of this change? Well, let's look at the timeline. Within just twelve years of losing his haberdashery (a loss that would have permanently dispirited many other men) Harry Truman was a United States Senator. And just over eleven years after entering the Senate, he found himself taking the oath of office as President of the United States.

On Truman's desk in the Oval Office, he placed a little sign that served as evidence of the new mental path he had blazed for himself back in 1922 – the mental path that had made his sales career, the Senate, the Presidency, and indeed an entirely different life, possible for him. The sign bore only four words, but it told visitors everything they needed to know about the "other" Harry Truman – the "new" man who had emerged from the rubble of not one, but seven failed careers.

The little sign read: "The Buck Stops Here."

Somehow, at a point in his life when he was a nobody, from

nowhere, in debt up to his eyeballs and pushing forty, Harry Truman found his "other self" – the self who was a Master.

"As Harry Truman, I'm not very much," he once said of himself, "but as President Truman, I have no peer." Of course, Harry Truman had actually located "President Truman" within himself long before he entered the White House. The question is, how did he do it?

Let me venture an answer by quoting the President himself. Once, when he was asked by a reporter about the topic of education, Mr. Truman gave a remarkable answer. It was the answer of a man who had seen failure close up, looked it over closely, and resolutely refused to allow it to define him.

You may be interested to learn about Mr. Truman's pragmatic definition of the concept of "education." Let me urge you to read his words on this subject closely, and to ponder their true meaning.

"Once you get a real education, that is something nobody can take from you. Money is only temporary - but what you have in your head, if you have the right kind of head, stays with you."

These potentially life-changing words may have more meaning to us if we recall that Harry Truman is the *only* U.S. President of the modern era to enter the White House with only a high-school diploma to his credit.

Yet who could possibly argue that he was uneducated? He had learned the one thing that is truly of critical importance: he had learned to *see* himself in way that made greatness a foregone conclusion, and he had learned, seemingly at the same time, to be *accountable* in a way that others weren't. *The buck really did stop at his desk.*

Does it stop at yours?

## The art of changing thought

Let's be blunt. If you want to be a Sales Master, you need to have a "millionaire mindset." That means *thinking like powerful and affluent people think.* This is a skill you must master, not a birthright you inherit. (In fact, it is such an important skill that I am making this chapter of the book, which addresses it, longer than all that follow it.)

The only way to obtain the mindset of the powerful and affluent is to do what Truman did – declare your independence from external forces and *hold yourself accountable.* In his own words:

> **"If I want to be great, I have to win the victory over myself through self-discipline."**

He did not complain about elusive oil wells or stores that went bust. He realized that he had to hold *himself* accountable, and no one else. This very realization is the key to Sales Mastery, and indeed all other forms of Mastery. It is the necessary preliminary to *summoning the Master within you.*

Once you hold yourself accountable, you will have no trouble committing (not wishing) to become affluent yourself, and *visualizing* yourself, with a burning desire, as already having attained your financial goal.

Yes, this takes mental effort. *The very effort will distinguish you from the vast majority of people who never attempt to summon their own inner Master, and indeed believe that no such Master exists.*

## The top salesperson

Can you see, hear, and experience yourself as the top salesperson in your organization?

You can. Right now. Start by changing the way you communicate with yourself internally.

*Use this metaphor:* You are not simply a salesperson. You're the owner. You're the president of You, Incorporated. You are currently sitting in your own personal Oval Office.

Nobody else on earth is going to do that job. If it's going to be done, you're going to have to take the initiative …. and do it yourself.

Once you get used to seeing yourself as the owner of "your" company – that is, your territory – then seeing yourself as the top sales agent is really no big deal.

## You already know how to do this

Believe it! You know how to summon the Master within yourself in a positive, optimistic, determined way.

Can you remember ONE time when you faced a major challenge in your life … and then overcame it? (Examples: getting a job, recovering from injury or illness, prevailing in/completing a sports event.)

Yes ____
No ____

What was the biggest obstacle you faced then?

_____

What did you learn about what you could really do?

_____

See, hear, and feel the way you overcame that challenge before you proceed any further in this book.

# Skill 2

## Using the Law of Commonality

### Principle #2: We already have something in common with the prospect

*"There's really no separation between the rapport that we feel when we're in conversation and the rapport we feel when we're playing music; it's one and the same."*

– Jazz legend Benny Green, on what makes for a good quartet.

R ead the sentence below out loud:

The Law of Commonality: **People want to do business with the people they LIKE ... and they really *love* doing business with people who are LIKE THEM.**

If you understand that simple principle, you will have no problem "getting" what Benny Green was *really* talking about in the quote above. It might *sound* like he was talking about jazz, but he was really talking about sales.

Don't we want the kind of relationship with a prospect where we simply "make beautiful music together?" Don't we want the trust to be implicit, and mutual? Don't we want the conversation to be effortless?

Of course we do. The question is, how do we make that happen? Here's the answer: By establishing commonality at the very beginning of the relationship, and by building upon it over time.

You can master the commonality piece with very little effort. *Start by writing The Law of Commonality in your own handwriting, and posting it someplace you can't possibly miss it. Read it out loud daily.*

## A misunderstood concept

Most salespeople misunderstand what is actually meant by "building rapport" in the sales process.

Do you want to know why that is?

It's because the managers, trainers, and authors we run into *let us down.* They tell us to "build rapport," but don't actually tell us what rapport *means*, so we don't really know how to build it. Fortunately, that stops here and now, with this chapter. If you're reading these words, you're about to all get the information you really need on the seemingly elusive skill of rapport-building. Ready?

**What is "rapport"?**

# The four facts of rapport-building

- *Fact #1:* You already have something in common with the person you're trying to sell to.

- *Fact #2:* Once you identify what that something is, and start talking about it, you're building rapport.

- *Fact #3:* If you haven't yet figured out what that "something" is, you are NOT building rapport.

- *Fact #4:* You cannot do ANYTHING ELSE in the sales process until you have established some kind of rapport.

# Rapport and commonality

Some salespeople tell me things like, "Of course I know how to build rapport – after all, people are always saying that I'm really good with people. How could I *not* know how to build rapport?"

What they mean is that they're really good at talking *at* people.

Most salespeople believe that mastering the art of conversation is

**Discussing a shared experience**

the *same* as mastering the art of building rapport. They are *not* the same. If you're moving your mouth and the person hasn't left the room, you're engaged in conversation ... but you may not have built up any meaningful rapport with the other person.

Sales Masters know when they're "just talking" ... and they know when they're building rapport. There are probably hundreds, thousands of times that you've used rapport-building to establish a new relationship. If you've ever asked for a date, or gotten a job offer, or exchanged high fives during a sporting event, then you have definitely built up rapport. That is, you've discussed a shared experience with one or more people you did not yet know.

Now, the point where *you* actually got the date, got the job offer, or made a new friend after giving someone a high five may have been just a short time after you established rapport ... or it may have been quite a long time after you first made that kind of connection. But the point is, whatever happened in the relationship, it happened by building on the *commonality* you had previously established with a person who used to be a stranger.

## You have more in common than you think!

The truth is, you *do* have something in common with the people who could buy from you. In fact, there are two basic categories of commonality you already know about. All I want to do is remind you of them.

**External and internal commonalities**

Let's start with *external commonalities*. These are going to vary with each person you meet, and they're going to vary with each circumstance you encounter. They could feature any one of the following manifestly **easy** topics of conversation:

· Whether there's a good place to eat nearby.

· Whether you and the other person lived in the same area at any point in time.

- Whether you and the other person studied anything similar in school.

- Whether you and the other person ever traveled to the same geographical area for any reason.

- And so on.

There are (at least) one thousand easy things like this that you *could* talk about with any person you're trying to sell to. In fact, if you think about it, you'll realize that this list could almost go on forever.

**Start small**

These are *easy entry points to any conversation*. And that's fortunate, because *some* kind of easy rapport-building based on *some* kind of external commonality *must* come at the very beginning of your sales cycle. You'll start with small commonalities (like the ones above) and work your way up to more meaningful ones. But you have to start!

If there is no commonality, there's no rapport; if there's no rapport, there's nothing for the other person to click on. You want your conversational partner to be able to think, "Hey, this person is like me. He's looking for a good place to eat around here, just like I was a while back"

**If there's no commonality, there's no rapport**

And if the other person *hasn't* found some connecting point, big or small, that says you're just like him or her in some way, then *you're not doing your job as a salesperson, and you have no right trying to move forward to any discussion of what you or your organization offer!*

Now we're ready to talk about the other half of the equation

... *internal commonality.* All of those external commonalities we just saw were setting up the one critical *internal* commonality. This is the most important commonality of all, the one that your meeting, conversation, or negotiation session is really all about, namely:

## You are both committed to turning goals into reality.

Now *there's* something good businesspeople love to talk about: their goals, and their habit of setting and attaining goals!

At some level ... don't you have this trait in common with every business contact that could conceivably do business with you? In fact ... don't *all* successful businesspeople have this trait in common?

Think about it. The weather. The commute. The sports team. All of those simple external commonalities are doing a single, essential job, namely, pointing you toward the one *incredibly* easy-to-talk-about *internal* commonality that you absolutely, positively, have in common with this person: **the fact that you are both goal-oriented.**

## Having a mission

Whether you and the prospect *share* the specific goals you're discussing doesn't matter all that much. What matters is that you and your prospect both understand, in your gut, that you're each concerned with the *business* of turning goals into tangible reality. That's the most important commonality there is!

## Passion sells

Do you have a goal that excites and inspires you, and connects to something powerful, enjoyable, and larger than yourself? One you can get passionate about? If so, you're ready to move on with the rest of this chapter.

If not, set that passion-inducing personal goal right now, and decide exactly when you want to attain it. (Remember: I said I was going to challenge you, as your coach. This is one of those challenges.) Fill in the blanks below by completing these three sentences.

*My chief aim in life is to ...*


*My goal is to accomplish or achieve this by a certain point in time, namely...*


*Right now, I can now see myself in possession of ...*


Have you got that goal and that timeline fixed in your mind? Can you see yourself already in possession of what you are committed to?

Great. You won't be *talking* about this goal with your prospects and customers ... but if you do not *have it,* you will not be able to establish commonality on the basis of your shared desire to transmute thoughts and ideas into tangible reality.

Right now, I want you to write your goal and its timeline down on a slip of paper – and I want you to post that slip of paper right next to the Law of Commonality in your workspace.

There are two "cults" in this world: The "cult" of people who take orders, and have no personal mission … and the "cult" of people who have a clear goal in life, and set their own agenda on their way to that goal. *Make the decision right now to join the "cult" of people who are on a mission in life.* Consider how easy it is to establish commonality and rapport with someone when you are members of the same "cult." Members of the "cult" of achievement can recognize, and connect with, fellow "cult members" … by means of something as simple as a nod or a glance! But you have to join up first!

## Evidence of effective rapport-building

You really can establish rapport and commonality. In fact, you already *are* doing it. You've actually been establishing rapport and talking with people about goals for years. But you may not have thought about what you were doing in these terms.

When you look back at the important relationships you've had in your life, isn't it true that they *all* started with external commonalities of some kind? As a result of shared experiences you discussed? And didn't the shared experiences eventually help create an important bond between the two of you? The person you were talking to built up an ability to trust you, because he or she concluded, "Hey, this person is like me in X area."

And didn't those external commonalities connect, eventually, to a *shared goal* that you were willing and able to discuss with that person? Didn't that discussion about goals improve the quality of the relationship?

Guess what? While all that was happening ... *you were working on your closing skills*, whether you realized it or not!

## Evidence of no rapport-building

Now let's look at the other side: Have you ever gotten to a second or third meeting with a prospect and heard the person say, "You know what – this really isn't right for us"? And at that point, have you ever thought to yourself, "Wow – how did that happen? Why in the world did I spend so much time on this proposal?"

Be honest with yourself: Has that *ever* happened?

I thought so. Do you know what that was? *That was proof that you did not talk about external AND internal commonalities during the first meeting!* If the person had gotten to a point where he or she had full rapport with you, trusted you, and shared his or her goals with you, you could easily have found out what, if anything, *was* "right" for that prospect ... right there at the first meeting! And you could have avoided building a presentation that ended up going nowhere.

> **"How did that happen?"**

Sometimes we confuse rapport-building (that is, finding, locating, and exploiting internal or external commonality) with the act of *flapping our jaws and listening to ourselves talk!* That's what most salespeople who *think* they're building rapport are actually doing: talking *at* people. Again: that's not rapport-building. That's giving a monologue!

If you've built up rapport with someone and established commonality, you can look the person in the eye and say, "Okay. What have we got here? How do we move this forward?" And you'll get a meaningful answer in return. *You can't close deals if you never establish rapport with the other person!*

## The hotel desk

Let me tell you a true story about a major national hotel chain. The senior management decided to put little badges on the chests of all the front-desk people. No exceptions. If you were someone responsible for greeting a guest at the front desk, you *had* to wear a little badge.

Can you guess what was on that badge?

The name and logo of the hotel, sure. But that wasn't all. The badge also showed first and last names of the front-desk person. Yes. But that wasn't all. What *else* was on the badge?

Drawing a blank? I'll tell you the answer. That badge always carried the name of the *home town of the person working the front desk*. Now, why would they go to the trouble of putting that on every badge? Because they knew a certain percentage of the hotel guests were going to be people who had tapped into their Inner Rapport Master. In short, the hotel knew that *people like you were going to be talking to that front desk person.*

**"You're from Peoria?"**

Think about it. A certain number of people encountering that front-desk person over the course of a year are, inevitably, going to be people who have *trained themselves* to build rapport with other people at every opportunity.

So picture this. The CEO of a Fortune 100 company checks in. He hands his credit card to the front desk attendant. As he does so, he notices that the front desk attendant is from Peoria, Illinois. By a remarkable coincidence, the CEO happens to be from a town near Peoria. The clerk and the CEO have a conversation about Peoria – and they establish (you guessed it) an *external commonality*.

Suppose the two of them connect in a strong way (internal commonality), and suppose the front desk attendant takes personal responsibility for ensuring that the CEO's stay is a pleasant one. Is that CEO now more likely, or less likely, to book all his future travel using that hotel?

Remember: *People want to do business with the people they LIKE ... and they really love doing business with people who are LIKE THEM.*

## You already know how to do this

Believe it! You know how to build rapport and commonality.

Can you remember ONE time when you built a new relationship with someone who seemed like a "stranger" you couldn't talk to – but turned out to be important in your life? (Examples: future spouse, future boss, future partner, future colleague.)

Yes ___
No ___

What was the biggest obstacle you faced in initially trying to communicate with this person?

_____

What finally happened?

_____

See, hear, and feel the way you built internal and external commonality with that person before you proceed any further in this book.

# Skill 3

## Getting Serious by Lightening Up

### Principle #3: Humor opens the magic window

*"You can pretend to be serious,
but you can't pretend to be witty."*
— Sacha Guitry, French film actor, director, and playwright.

**W**hy should you make a point of using humor in your sales process? Because humor is the greatest social lubricant known to humankind. Humor releases closed interpersonal "windows." If the other person's "window" is clamped securely shut, *nothing can happen* in the sales process. But if the window opens even slightly, thanks to appropriate humor, suddenly possibility beckons.

49

The salesperson's intelligent use of humor often marks the difference between a deal that dies and one that closes. If you're skeptical about this, ask the top sales performer in your own organization about whether humor makes a difference. You'll quickly learn that the right humor can open the "magic window" – and you'll learn that humor can bring you to the point when things can really start to get *serious* between you and the prospect.

**Humor makes great things possible**

Let me be clear on one point: I'm not talking about turning you into a perpetual backslapper, a joke machine, or a performance artist. I'm talking about using humor strategically and appropriately. The *right* story or remark, told at the *right* time, really can move your sale process forward – and bring a smile to even the most stony-faced prospect.

Here's why.

## Humor means confidence

Humor shows people exactly how much you believe in yourself. Humor bespeaks confidence ... and confidence begets competence.

An appropriate, funny remark communicates your confidence in a powerful way. When you use humor in support of your goals (and especially when you use self-deprecating humor), you send this unspoken message: "I know enough about what I'm doing to poke fun at what's happening here – and at myself." That's a vitally important message for you to send to the prospect, because *full confidence in your goals is an essential part of Sales Mastery.* In a very real sense, using humor means taking control of the sales process.

If you do not have sufficient confidence in yourself and what you're doing to use humor now and then, it's almost certain that your life goal is still something you are only "wishing for," and not yet a burning obsession that melts away all obstacles. **If you cannot step back and tell a funny story about yourself from time to time, that means your confidence is still low, and your mission's conclusion is not yet a tangible reality within your mind.**

## Humor means goal orientation

When you can stake your entire personality on the pursuit of your own mission, you can easily place your entire personality behind the task of telling a funny story. In an odd, elusive, but undeniable way, the ability to use humor with prospects connects to your own ability to commit to your goal.

By the way – did you write down your sales goal, as you and I discussed together in the previous chapter … or did you maintain your objectivity by "waiting" and doing nothing for right now?

## He who waits is lunch.

If you chose to "wait," and are planning to write your goal down "later," let me respectfully suggest to you that this strategy can backfire.

Consider the case of the crow that was famous for sitting on a tree, waiting all day long for the right moment to take flight. One day a small rabbit happened by, saw the crow, and shouted up to him: "You've built up quite a reputation for doing nothing. Can I do what you're doing – wait around for inspiration to hit me, and

**The parable of the crow**

do nothing all day long?" The crow answered: "Go ahead." Delighted, the rabbit took a seat in the dirt directly below where the crow was perched, and waited for the right moment to come along. "I like this," the rabbit said. "The crow has got it all figured out. This is certainly a relaxing way to live." At that moment, a fox appeared, jumped on the rabbit, and gobbled him up in a single bite.

And the "business" moral of the story is: if you want to sit around and do nothing … you had better be sitting very high up.

Don't wait.

Know your goal.

Starting today.

If you're truly committed to your goal … and willing to talk about it … you'll benefit from this chapter's insights on using humor in your sales process. If you're *not* willing to do identify your goal and talk about it, the joke's on you. You're basically someone's lunch. Only you don't know it yet.

## Humor gets the topic of money "on the table"

I think every "good" salesperson on earth would agree with the following statement: Raising the issue of price can be a delicate matter.

That's true, but if you're going to close business, you've *got* to get the subject of money on the table with the people you're talking to, and you've got to make them feel comfortable discussing pricing with you. Humor is an indispensable tool for doing that.

Consider these two "big" conversational topics: money and sex. Of those two perennially interesting subjects, which one do you think people are more comfortable discussing with a stranger? If you thought it was money, think again. In discussions with someone

**What are the two big topics?**

they don't know, people turn out to be *much* more likely to start sharing intimate details about their private lives than they are to share the simplest details about their financial situation.

The reality is, when it comes to money, people get serious and tighten up. Whenever you see that happening, or suspect it is about to happen, you have to balance it with humor.

Scientific research has demonstrated that laughter boosts the human immune system, releases endorphins, and promotes a healthier lifestyle. My own research over the years with salespeople proves that laughter also boosts commissions: I firmly believe that the other person's endorphins have to fire off in order for him or her to trust you.

So use humor to break down the money barrier. After all, the first discussion about what they or their

**Open the "magic window"**

organizations can really afford is likely to be awkward. Awkward is the *opposite* of what you want!

To close the deal, you've got to get the topic of money on the table in a way that will open up the "magic window" and make a relaxed dialogue possible.

## Consider these dialogues

Suppose you've put together a pricing estimate for your prospect. How can you use humor to make the first dialogue about price go more smoothly – and open up that "magic window"? Here are some ideas.

*Prospect: We've got a problem with the price.*

*Sales Master Julia: (Deadpan, maintaining eye contact, and not missing a beat:) You know, I was afraid of that. Is it too low?*

**The defenses are down – the "magic window" is open!**

Here's another example.

*Prospect: Is your price negotiable?*

*You: Yes. Absolutely.*

**The defenses are down – the "magic window" is open!**

*You: How much more did you want to offer?*

So what happens then? The other person says, "Very funny. That's not what I was thinking… what I meant was …"

Then they start talking about how much they want to pay. But they're having a little fun now, and the emotional weather in the room has changed. That's what matters! We've demonstrated confidence – and we've gotten the money issue on the table without sabotaging the conversation.

Here's another example.

*Prospect: Don't get me wrong. I love the policy. It's what I want to do — it's just too darn expensive. You guys are just way beyond what my budget is. I don't even feel like negotiating with you — this is way out of my league.*

*You: I understand. Let me recommend some cheap stuff for you. You don't mind going cheap, do you?*

*Prospect: Well … uh … what did you have in mind?*

*You: I do have a 28-day policy.*

*Prospect: A 28-day policy? What's that?*

*You: Well, it's a policy that's literally half the price of the one we're looking at now.*

*Prospect: Why didn't you show me that before? What's the deal?*

*You: Well, let me tell you how it works. The reason it's called a 28-day policy is, you pick the 28 days out of the month you want to be insured. And then the other days of the month, you're open to the risk.*

*Prospect (laughing): Well, heck, with my luck, I'd die on the day I wasn't insured!*

*You: Exactly. That's why I didn't show it to you.*

---

**The defenses are down – the "magic window" is open!**

## Practice, practice, practice

You will be best at telling stories you're very familiar with. That's why it's important to practice them ahead of time, preferably with people who *aren't* your prospects. If you're looking for material, here are some good World Wide Web sites to mine for laughs:

*www.basicjokes.com*
*www.myhumor.org/business.asp*
*www.comedy-zone.net/jokes/*

Now, having shared those resources with you, let me make a very, very important point: don't rely on them too much. In fact, it's better not to rely on them at all. *Your own brand of humor is always going to be better than anyone else's, and truth is always going to be better than fiction.* If you've got the choice, use a genuinely amusing story from your own life before you using someone else's story. Keep an eye out for material from your own life ... and hone that material over time. Pretty soon, you won't just have a batch of *funny* stories ... you'll have a batch of *signature* stories.

## Humor to avoid

Stay away from humor involving race, cultural differences, religion, sex, or anything else that seems remotely questionable. If you have even the shadow of a doubt as to whether a story is appropriate, stay away from it.

Sexual innuendoes can be particularly dangerous, and can lead to legal problems for you and/or your company. In recent years, our ratings-driven media has sometimes made it seem like sex is okay as a form of business-related comedy material in the real world. No matter what you may have seen on *Sex and the City*, though, sex is *not* okay as a topic for workplace humor.

## Self-deprecating humor

Self-deprecating humor is the most effective kind there is.

This kind of humor shows that you're for real, and that you don't take yourself too seriously. It lets you acknowledge, and poke fun at, your own vulnerabilities. It shows that you're confident and mature enough to make yourself the target of your own wit. This kind of humor is a nearly universal trait of truly confident people.

Here's an example of the power of self-deprecating humor. In the 1984 presidential election, Ronald Reagan's opponent, Walter Mondale, had only one real chance to undercut the president's immense popularity with the American people: Reagan's age. Political pundits of all persuasions pointed to Reagan's advanced years, and his supposed mental decline, as his Achilles' heel.

Do you remember how President Reagan dealt with that challenge? During one of their live televised debates, Reagan showed that he still had enough on the ball to tell a joke on himself. He was asked directly about the supposedly devastating "age issue":

> *Mr. President, I want to raise an issue that I think has been lurking out there for two or three weeks, and cast it specifically in national security terms.*
>
> *You already are the oldest President in history, and some of your staff say you were tired after your most recent encoun-*

*ter with Mr. Mondale. I recall, yes, President Kennedy had
to go for days on end with very little sleep during the Cuba
missile crisis. Is there any doubt in your mind that you
would be able to function in such circumstances?*

Reagan's response to this pointed question was masterful. With
untold millions of people watching, he said simply:

*I will not make age an issue of this campaign. I am not
going to exploit, for political purposes, my opponent's youth
and inexperience.*

America laughed … and made up its mind. Game, set, and
match – and election – to the Great Communicator!

## You already know how to do this

Believe it! Humor demonstrates confidence ... opens up the "magic window" ... and creates opportunities for essential communication with the people who make decisions. Even if you aren't a born "stand-up comic," you really have found opportunities to share a laugh with someone who was important to you ... and that laughter broke down barriers that altered the situation for the better.

Can you remember ONE adult you have laughed out loud with who was not a blood relative?

Yes \_\_\_\_

No \_\_\_\_

If yes, who was that person?

_____

What made you both laugh?

_____

Before you move on to the next chapter, ponder this question: **What did you do to help make that moment of fun connection possible?**

# Skill 4

## Unlocking the Intuitive Power of People-Reading

### Principle #4: Follow your instinct

*"Learn to reveal something of yourself. To get others
to open up, you must first open up to them."*

– Jo-Ellan Dimitrius and Mark C. Mazzarella, authors, *Reading People:
How to Understand People* and *Predict Their Behavior – Anytime, Anyplace*

When we first meet them, prospects have a shield around them. Our job is to help them dissolve that shield.

This chapter is all about using your "gut instincts" as a tool for dissolving the shield … and figuring out what's really important to the other person.

## It's easy to use this ...today!

This is not a new skill you're going to have to develop from scratch before you can expect to close the next deal. It's an *existing* skill you can take full advantage of *right now.* You can use it during your very next conversation with a suspect, prospect, or customer.

## Reality check

Isn't it true that, at various points in your life, you've been in situations where you could just *sense* that someone was really "clicking" with you? And isn't it true that, as a result of sensing that, you *felt very, very good* about taking the initiative to move the relationship forward in some tangible way?

Of course you've had that experience. Get specific about one of those times that this took place. Review it in your mind right now.

Now, I want you to think of the specific person that that experience connected to. Do your best to **visualize that person's face, feel what it's like to be with that person, and hear that person's voice, right now.**

## Empathic intelligence

When that experience happened – when you followed your instinct and got that "someone" to agree to go on a date with you, or loan you twenty bucks, or give you the (precious!) name and phone number of an *honest* auto mechanic in your city – when you got someone to agree to do one of those things, or anything like them, you were making full use of a skill I call *empathic intelligence.* It's an intuitive sense of what matters, and will matter, to someone else.

Now let's dig a little deeper. Do you know *why* you had that impossible-to-ignore sense that the other person was "clicking" with you ... *before* you asked for the date, or asked for the twenty bucks, or asked for the contact information for the auto mechanic?

**It all comes together**

I'll tell you why. Because, prior to that point, you'd established *commonality and rapport* with that person! You'd given them a reason to say, "Hey, this person is like me" about **some specific thing that you had in common.**

(Wow. It's all starting to come together, isn't it?)

## What if there had been nothing in common?

Think about it. If you *hadn't* established commonality and rapport with the other person, would he or she have given you the date? Loaned you the twenty bucks? Given you the phone number that every auto owner within a ten-mile radius would have killed for? No way!

Now here's another piece of the puzzle that's about to fall into place. Once you had established commonality and rapport, *you shared something specific about yourself with that other person, something that was important to you.* Right?

Right!

Maybe you told the person you wanted to ask out on a date about a life goal that was very meaningful to you as a person – and your special "someone" was able to see that goal as being fulfilled, based on what you said, did, and experienced with them. Maybe you told the person how important it was to you as a person of integrity to repay the loan on time, and you helped them to "experience" that repayment before it actually took place. Maybe, before you asked for the name of that auto mechanic, you talked with the other person about your common passion for classic Corvettes, and got the person to visualize what it actually would be like to drive your favorite automobile.

I don't know specifically what happened in your world, but I do know this: You shared *something* about yourself! You had to! In fact, you may even have shared something that was of *burning importance to you ... something that you and the other person somehow experienced together as "real" – before it was a tangible reality.*

But somewhere along the line, you had to share *something* about yourself – after all, people aren't in the habit of loaning money to complete strangers, or giving them important information. And then, in all likelihood, you *learned* something important about the other person.

## The "magic formula" for people reading

Here's the three-step formula for unlocking your intuitive ability to read people like a book:

1. Share something. Stop talking. Learn something.

2. Share something else. Stop talking. Learn something else.

**The people-reading formula**

3. Repeat steps 1 and 2 as necessary.

If you practice this consciously, as opposed to by doing it by instinct, a remarkable thing will start to happen. You will actually start to develop a "gut feeling" for what is *about* to be important to the other person! *How this happens, no person can truly say ... but that it happens is undeniable.*

In sales, this process of arriving at an instinctive decision about the other person's true priorities is absolutely critical. It's where the real Sales Masters stand out from salespeople who are merely "good."

So: Did you buy this book just to get "good" at closing? Or do you want to be *great*?

I thought so. Then you're ready for what comes next.

## Use focus to improve your instincts

There is a price to pay for the Sales Master's instinctive ability to read people's priorities. We must *stop talking and focus with absolutely undivided attention on the other person.* Here's how it breaks down for those who wish to **Close and Grow Rich.**

Note that the type size and box thinkness on the following pages suggests how much time you will, ideally, want to spend in each step of the interaction.

## Move toward the thicker lined boxes!

1. **BEGINNING COMMONALITY.** Together, you establish commonality and rapport (about external things like the weather, the local sports team, whatever). YOU PAY UNDIVIDED ATTENTION WHEN THE OTHER PERSON SPEAKS.

2. **ADVANCED COMMONALITY.** Together, you establish MORE commonality and rapport (this time about internal matters, specifically your shared willingness to focus on and achieve important goals. These should be goals that are so important to you that they get you excited when you talk about them. (Note: This is NOT a monologue!)

3. **INITIATIVE.** Now you take the lead and BRIEFLY outline a specific BROAD goal that a) benefits the other person, b) drives you, c) is something you can and do envision right now as reality, and d) is so important to you that it gets you excited when you talk about it. (Again, this is NOT a monologue, but a few sentences. You then SHUT UP and see what the other person says in response, and what that tells you about what's important to him or her. YOU PAY UNDIVIDED ATTENTION WHEN THE OTHER PERSON SPEAKS.)

4. **BEGINNING FEEDBACK FROM THE PROSPECT.** The other person responds at greater length and in greater detail than you used about the goal you've just identified. You listen and take notes. You DO NOT interrupt the other person. YOU PAY UNDIVIDED ATTENTION WHEN THE OTHER PERSON SPEAKS.

5. **SPECIFICITY.** Now YOU go into more detail about a somewhat NARROWER version of the same goal, one that comes closer to the goal of "fitting like a glove" to the other person's situation. You then ask if you're on the "same page" with the other person.

6. **ADVANCED FEEDBACK FROM THE PROSPECT.** The other person should answer in detail and at length, not in vague or one-syllable terms. You should be listening for a longer period of time than you were just talking, and getting a clearer intuitive fix on what's important to this person. YOU PAY UNDIVIDED ATTENTION WHEN THE OTHER PERSON SPEAKS.

If you practice that pattern – the one you just read – just as I've described it, you'll soon be in a position where you'll truly "sense," at a gut level, that you've really clicked with the other person. You'll be in no doubt whatsoever as to what's on the prospect's agenda.

(Note: See Skill #10, *Clear the Decks,* for a fuller discussion of the power of undivided attention in your sales process.)

## The power of pronesia

Let me tell you a true story about a gentleman named Jim that I met in Myrtle Beach, South Carolina at one of my seminars. During the program, Jim mentioned a great term from classical literature for this ability to "read people" that Sales Masters possess – this ability to share something, learn something, and, eventually, instinctively anticipate what's *about* to be important.

He called it "pronesia," as in the opposite of amnesia (losing one's memory). **Pronesia means actually gaining the ability to understand what will matter in the future.** Empathic intelligence is what pronesia is all about: the instinctive ability to read another person's agenda quickly, accurately, and with a strong sense of where things are going. True Sales Masters are very, very good at this improvisational, "empathic" part of the job. Ultimately, as author Malcolm Gladwell points out in his fine book *Blink,* interpersonal effectiveness is a matter of learning to open oneself to one's surroundings, and then acting upon one's initial instincts.

> **What's *going* to be important?**

To learn more about the way top performers learn to honor these "hunches" about where things are really going … how they think about and experience the job of selling itself … and how they use their own "internal messaging system" to develop the full person-to-person connection that makes "pronesia" possible … see my book *What's Your Sales DNA?* (Or visit www.MySalesDNA.com.)

## Science weighs in

A recent scholarly article on the topic of intuition reads as follows:

"The most brilliant decisions tend to come from the gut. ... (That observation) is now backed by a growing body of research from economics, neurology, cognitive psychology, and other fields. What the science suggests is that intuition – or instinct, or hunch, or 'learning without awareness,' or whatever you want to call it – is a real form of knowledge. It may be irrational, ineffable, and not always easy to get in touch with, but it can process more information on a more sophisticated level than most of us ever dreamed. Psychologists now say that far from being the opposite of effective decision-making, intuition is inseparable from it." – *Thomas A. Stewart, "Think with Your Gut," p. 99 (November 2002)*

## You already know how to do this

Believe it! You do know how to read people, and you know when to ask directly for a commitment.

Can you think of a time in your life when you knew instinctively that something "wasn't right" in your conversation with someone – so you held back and did not push for something you had meant to ask for?

Yes _____
No _____

Can you think of a time in your life when everything was "clicking" – when you felt like you'd known someone forever, and felt totally comfortable about moving the relationship forward in a tangible way?

Yes _____
No _____

What was the common thread between those two experiences?

_____

# Skill 5

## Establish an Unfair Advantage

### Principle #5: Defend yourself against "so what"?

*"Determine exactly what you intend to give in return for the money you desire. There is no such reality as something for nothing."*

– Napoleon Hill, author of *Think and Grow Rich*

In any selling situation, there's an internal monologue going on within the prospect. That monologue starts with the two "dirtiest" words a salesperson can hear: *So what?*

If you don't do your job, those words will cross your prospect's mind. Your prospect is always on the verge of thinking (or perhaps even saying) *so what?*

Stop right now and think about the prospects in your world. Are they saying that? If they're not saying that out loud, are they thinking it?

Now here's the big question: *What are you going to do to keep them from using language like that? Wash their mouths out with soap?*

Some people seem to think the best response to that spoken or unspoken "So what?" is the *organization's* take on the Unique Selling Proposition. In other words, they want the salesperson to sim-

**The two dirtiest words**

ply repeat the familiar catch-phrase that the good folks in that committee up in Corporate came up with a year and a half ago. It might sound like this: "We put the customer first." Or it might sound like this: "Success, one project at a time." Or it might sound like this: "We do whatever it takes." Snore.

Obediently chanting some overworked marketing catch-phrase when the prospect is likely to be thinking "So what?" is a big, big mistake. Why? Because it overlooks everything that's unique about the prospect's world ... and it also overlooks everything that's unique about you and your world.

In this chapter, you will acknowledge that this kind of skepticism from the prospect really does operate in your world. (It does.) And you will develop two powerful defenses against "So what?"

## The Unique Selling Proposition

Most salespeople think they understand the principle of the "unique selling proposition." They are already comfortable thinking about a single, simple sentence that supposedly distinguishes their product or organization from all the "other guys." They may memorize that corporate marketing catch-phrase. Some salespeople may even say that sentence out loud once or twice during the course of a year.

That's not what I'm talking about in this chapter. I'm talking about something very different, something that you can use as an *unfair advantage* over the "other guys." I'm talking about something that's "covert," something that can make you one of the 20% of the organization's sales force that accounts for 80% of the actual income.

What I'm talking about in this chapter is a creating a "triple whammy" that can protect you ahead of time against "So what?"

## The "Triple Whammy"

The "Triple Whammy" is a three-tiered Unique Selling Proposition that identifies what *actually* distinguishes:

- Your organization

- Your product

- You

from the competition.

Notice the wording we're using: what *actually* distinguishes you from the competition, in *each* of these three areas? When I work with sales teams, I will ask them directly whether they've got a Unique Selling Proposition in one or more of these areas. Everyone in the room will insist that the answer is "yes." Then I'll call on someone and say, "Sam, tell me the Unique Selling Proposition that connects to your product." Sam will say, "We offer a money-back guarantee on everything we ship."

Then I'll say to the group, "Okay, that's interesting. Does any-one *else* in this industry offer a money-back guarantee on every-thing that's shipped?"

There will be a little silence, and then someone will say, "Well, yeah, actually, Acme offers a money-back guarantee. And so does Boswell. And so does Cardigan. And so does ...."

And on it goes. That's when I have to reinforce a key point: *unique means unique.*

In each of these three areas, you have to identify something that the consumer will find *nowhere else on earth.* Take a look at this Triple Whammy – and ponder the unfair advantage that knowing something like this inside and out would give you over the competition.

- *YOUR COMPANY: What really sets us apart is that we have, by unanimous consent, the very best customization team in the industry; in fact, we were named by a leading trade magazine as hav-ing the "most accomplished redesign and custom-ization staff in North America." If you're trying to make sure a project absolutely, positively fits your organization like a glove, we are flat-out the best people in the country to do that for you.*

- *THE PRODUCT: I'll tell you frankly that this item is perceived as the most expensive on the mar-ket, but I want you to know why we feel that's not really accurate. We decided years ago that we sim-ply could not compromise on quality. Our philoso-phy is this: If, two years down the line, you have to replace a unit or spend a lot of money to have it re-paired, you probably didn't get the best deal. When*

*you look at its cost of ownership, this actually turns
out to be the very best value on the market. And
that's not according to us – that's what Consumer
Reports had to say about the machine.*

- *YOU: I'm looking forward to working with you
on this project, and it's been a real pleasure to meet
with you today. My name is Palumbo – John Palumbo – like Columbo, the detective who was on
TV back in the Seventies.*

Each of these distinctive elements they outline simply cannot
be connected to the "other guys." Each of them earns *top-of-mind
awareness* in the prospect's world.

Whatever amount of time and effort it takes you to develop
a three-tiered "defense system" like the one you just read, you
should make the investment. Notice, with benefit, that most of
the salespeople you'll be competing against will create a statement
about the product, but make little or no effort to come up with
USP's that connect to the *organization* or *the salesperson*. If they do
take the trouble to create something for their organization, it will
sound like this: "We offer high quality and great service at a value
price." *Virtually everyone on earth is saying that!* There's nothing
memorable about it. By the same token, salespeople say things
about themselves like, "I've been with the company 25 years, and I
have X, Y, and Z, experience." *That's what any salesperson could say!*
To achieve top-of-mind dominance, you must create something
memorable that connects to *you as a person.* You can do this in any
number of ways, including drawing attention to something that
rhymes with your name ... or passing along a saying, philosophy,
or piece of advice that connects to you and you alone ... or even

by drawing attention to some physical characteristic the prospect is unlikely to forget once you make reference to it. Once, I was shopping for furniture, and the salesperson who had been talking to me smiled and said, "You go ahead and take a look around ... if you need anything, just ask for the *shortest salesperson in the store.*" He was indeed about five foot two, and he was obviously proud of it! I ended up tracking him down using exactly the method he had suggested, namely, by asking for the shortest salesperson in the store! He got a sizeable commission from my purchase that day. What I want you to notice, though, is that he said his little tag-line about asking for the *shortest person in the store* to me five years ago! Not only do I remember the tag-line, I still remember *him*, and still buy furniture from him!

Let's look now at your second secret weapon against "so what."

## What are the benefits of the benefit?

"Good" salespeople know how to sell features and benefits in tandem – any basic sales training program will make that point clearly enough. Suppose for a moment that you're in the real estate business, and you're showing a home with a pool to a prospective buyer. You wouldn't simply talk about the depth of the pool – you'd connect that feature to a particular benefit the homeowner might experience. So, for instance, you might say: "*Because* the pool is fourteen feet deep at its far end, it's great for diving, which adds life to pool parties and, perhaps, a new level of interest to personal swimming sessions."

That's what a *good* salesperson knows how to do: tie the feature to a benefit. But how about a *great* salesperson?

The Sales Master will tie the benefit *itself* to another benefit. So in this case, the Master might say:

"The pool here is fourteen feet deep on this end. [That's a feature.] That means it's great for diving, which really livens up a pool party and makes solo exercise a little more interesting. [That's a benefit.] But the thing I really like about the diving and the pool parties is the stress relief. [That's a benefit of a benefit!] Taking a dive into this end of the pool is just a great way to fast-forward past everything that happened at the office during the course of the day. In fact, a lot of people in the neighborhood have told me that they're now very big on diving, not just swimming – they've really reduced their overall stress, improved the quality of their family time, and brought their quality of life to a whole different level. [That's where following the benefit of the benefit ends up leading you – to an improved quality of life.]"

## Treat goals as accomplished realities

A Sales Master knows how to treat the partner's goals as *accomplished realities*. And that's what selling the benefit of the benefit is all about. To do this, you focus on a unique *extension* of the benefit – something the benefit itself *delivers,* something the prospect can't get anywhere else. This "extended" benefit should be chosen specifically for *this person*. It should be something you personally identify and communicate with passion ... and the full belief that the person might as well begin to enjoy it right now.

Until you put these two weapons to work .... until you create a "triple whammy" proposition that illuminates what the prospect can get *only* from working with you ... until you learn to summon the "benefits of the benefit" with power and energy, and treat them as accomplished realities … you're on an equal footing with your competition! Nothing will stand out! No decisions will be made! Until you establish an unfair advantage, the prospect will be playing (and replaying) a familiar song on his or her mental jukebox: *So What?*

## A True Story

My daughter was in the market for a car recently. She noticed (as you may have noticed, if you've ever purchased a new car) that each of the automobiles on the lot was slightly different. You don't look at eight identical cars. You look at eight cars that may be the same model, but that are tricked out and equipped slightly differently. Now that you've read this chapter, you should be able to describe exactly why that is.

Can you?

Right. The cars are slightly different so that the salesperson can make a unique appeal to a particular prospect: "I can just see you with the sun roof down, listening to the satellite radio, with the volume pumped up all the way." And by the way, that's the only unit on the lot that has both a sun roof and satellite radio! While there are eight cars on the lot that look identical from a distance, each of them has a Unique Selling Proposition tailored specifically to that car. Once you, the buyer, hook into a specific proposition for a specific car, that car starts to glow, and all the others on the lot start to get dim. A small advantage over another vehicle becomes a very *big* reason to buy.

In case you were wondering … yes, my daughter's new car has a sun roof and a satellite radio.

## You already know how to do this

Believe it! You do know how to give yourself an unfair advantage over "the other guys."

Can you remember ONE person in your life to whom you made a "one-of-a-kind" proposition that the person accepted? (Note: This could be in a business setting, or it could be something you said to a close friend, or it could even be a proposal of marriage.)

Yes  _____
No  _____

If yes, who was that person?

_____

What did this person agree to do?

_____

Before you move on to the next chapter, ponder these questions: *What did you help the other person to experience before it came into reality? How did you do that?*

# Skill 6

## Using the Velvet Hammer

### Principle #6: Build Pressure from Within

*"Your prospect buys because you have hit on some very strong emotion he already possesses."*
– Will Newman, advertising and copywriting guru

You could work for weeks, or months, or even years to "convince" your prospect, logically, that what you have to offer is a great idea. But if your by-the-numbers *logic* is the force leading the discussion, you will almost always lose out to the "other guys."

If you wish to *Close and Grow Rich*, you must identify the *emotion* involved in the other person's world ... and you must find subtle ways to act upon that emotion.

I call this process of engaging emotionally with the prospect, and acting tactically on the emotions you kindle, "using the Velvet Hammer." It's "velvet" because it's soft and comfortable and already quite familiar to the prospect. It's a "hammer" because, even though you don't create the emotion in question ... you do "strike hard" to take advantage of an emotional reaction that's already there. What you're really doing is building pressure from within.

**The only "pressure" that works**

This is the only "pressure" that ever accomplishes anything in a sales situation – internal pressure.

## Emotional involvement

Closing is all about emotional involvement. I'm talking about the kind of connection that allows you to guide the prospect to experience something that has not yet taken place, but can only take place as a result of this discussion with you.

As we saw in the previous chapter, this means breaking out of the usual, boring discussions – "Here's a feature, here's a benefit" – and moving toward something unique to this prospect, something he or she simply can't get anywhere else. Stake out those benefits and "drill for oil!"

Eventually, one of the "benefits of the benefits" that you raise will elicit an emotional response from the other person. That's an oil strike! Your job is then to a) notice when that happens, b) notice exactly what kind of emotion rises to the surface, and c) reinforce that emotion to build internal pressure for action.

## Beyond the "hard sell"

Understand: What I mean by "pressure" is something little that grows into something big. It's something that builds from within – as opposed to pressure from the outside, the classic "hard sell," which is merely a vise grip that squeezes and squeezes. One popular example of imporperly applied pressure is "I'm only offering this special today." That's not a very sophisticated selling approach, and it certainly doesn't guide the Sales Masters who *Close and Grow Rich*.

**Don't just squeeze**

In fact, effective use of "pressure" is something most salespeople simply don't understand. We're so used to thinking about "pressure" as something that a salesperson applies *externally* that we lose sight of what we really need to do, which is understand what's already operating. I'll give you an example.

Lots of salespeople ask me for a list of specific "closing questions" that can wrap up the sales process. There is no such list, and never can be! Why?

Because we as salespeople always have to focus in on the prospect like a laser beam and respond authentically to what the person *just said*. If we're thinking about what question we're supposed to say next, we can't do that!

## "What's Going On?"

Do you remember the famous Marvin Gaye song, "What's Going On?" It's a key to understanding this principle.

Joe Smith walks onto the showroom of a local car dealer. A true Sales Master won't put external "pressure" on him to buy one model over another ... instead, that Sales Master will find out what's going on right now in Joe's world.

Specifically, that Sales Master will want to know what car he's driving now and what's motivating the decision to even look at a new car. If you don't know that, you can't sell, because you don't yet know enough about Joe to build up any meaningful internal pressure! Without *that* kind of pressure, nothing's going to happen. The old saying really does hold true: In that sense, at least, the old saying holds true: "No pressure, no diamonds."

What is Joe driving right now? What is his discontentment? (If he is in the showroom, he is unhappy with *something*. What is it?) What's working? What's not? Make no mistake: Joe and his wife Mary are actively trying to change the situation, or even considering changing it, there's some pain, some reason for that. And if you as a salesperson don't know what that is, you're in trouble. If you try to close Joe and Mary before you know "*What's Going On,*" you will usually lose!

There's really no syllable-for-syllable checklist of the specific words you need to memorize to figure out what's going on in Joe's world. You have to be able to gauge whether you're involving Joe emotionally. But here's a simple overview of the basic questions you should be able to expand upon:

- Who is Joe? What does he do for a living?

- What's working in what Joe is currently using?

- When did Joe use something else?

- Where and with whom did Joe do that?

- How did it work out for Joe?

- Why is Joe using what he's using now?

That's what you need to understand at the outset. Once you've got that much, you're off and running, because you now have a sense of who the person is, and you can start "drilling for oil." You've got a little emotional involvement going – not a blank stare attached to a purchase order or a checkbook.

## A true story

Motivational master Anthony Robbins trains his sales team – the folks who are responsible for selling high-end tickets to Robbins's supercharged *Personal Power* and *Date with Destiny* events – to guide prospects through a process of visualization that emphasizes benefits they have not yet experienced. So for instance, at the end of a session, the Robbins sales consultant might ask if the prospect has kids.

If the answer is "Yes, I've got a twelve-year-old boy," the consultant might ask about the quality of communication the prospect presently has with that child. The conversation would then follow the prospect's lead, and the consultant might learn that the communication between the child and the parent hasn't been too great lately, since the family is going through a divorce.

> **"Picture yourself spending quality time with your kid..."**

"What," the consultant asks, "will be the consequences of leaving that relationship the way it is? One year from now, is it possible that the teenager will be spending time with people who don't share your values?" What would happen in two years' time, if the parent does nothing to improve the communication pattern? What about three years down the line? What kind of person will the adolescent have become five years from now, with all the values and habits of the "wrong crowd"? The Robbins sales consultant gets very, very good at helping people develop compelling, powerful pictures to accompany these tough "gut check" questions. (Obviously, you can't ask questions like that and expect to get meaningful answers if you don't first develop commonality and build rapport. The Robbins folks are great at that, too.)

Now that the "pain" is in place – removing it is simple. The consultant says, more or less: "Now picture yourself communicating better with your kid, bonding with him, spending more quality time with him." Which future is more compelling? The one where your kid spends time with the "wrong crowd" – or the one where he spends time with you? No question – as parents, we all want that second option.

So how do you make it happen? That's the easy part: "A weekend with Anthony Robbins, in person, can deliver – among many other benefits – tools for bonding and communication that will totally transform your relationship with your kids." (P.S.: That's absolutely true!) So, here's the question: is the prospect ready to take the action necessary to make that second future a reality?

**The deal is done**

Do you see what these industry leaders are doing? They're building up internal pressure ... and then applying the Velvet Hammer at precisely the spot where emotion already exists, the spot where they really can deliver a powerful, memorable benefit to the prospect! Once the prospect experiences that internally, and with emotion ... the deal is done!

## You already know how to do this

Believe it! You really do know how to use the "Velvet Hammer."

Can you think of ONE person in your life whom you helped to accomplish something that was really, really important to him or her? (Note: This could be a colleague you convinced to let you make a contribution in a business setting, or it could be a close friend, or it could even be a family member.)

Yes _____
No _____

If yes, who was that person?

_____

What did this person agree to let you do?

_____

Before you move on to the next chapter, ponder these questions: *What OUTCOME did you help the other person to experience BEFORE it came into reality? How did you do that?*

# Skill 7

## Take Baby Steps

### Principle #7: Start small

*"Life is so short that we must move very slowly."*
– Thai proverb

**C**losing deals like a Sales Master involves mastering a strange-sounding rule. This rule typically mystifies "good" salespeople ... but it is second nature for the truly great ones. If you began reading this book in order to become *great,* you're now ready to get your head around this idea. Here it is:

---

**To close any big deal, you must first close a small one.**

---

89

Maybe you're thinking, "People close big deals all the time without closing small ones."

Do we really? Or do we win a lot of small commitments *before* we win a big one? (Like, for instance, the commitment to meet with someone in the first place?) Do we secure little, preliminary buy-ins on seemingly minor issues – commitments that, over time, gather a cumulative force in the relationship, and result in wins for everyone?

We are too easily distracted, I think, by the myth that "closing" is something that happens at the end of the sales process. "Closing" actually starts long before you have any interaction with the prospect. It starts in your own mind. If you think of the person as a buyer, before you even shake hands with him or her, you're on the right track. That person then *is* a buyer to you. If you *don't* think of the person as a buyer before you shake hands, you are not yet a Sales Master.

You must, in your mind, turn the person into a buyer long before you ask for the business … indeed, before you ask for any commitment whatsoever, or say a single word to the prospect … I mean, buyer.

## You read right!

It's no joke. The connection must happen in your mind *first*. After you've done that, your job is to make it easy for the prospect to start *experiencing* that reality you've created within your mind.

Guess what? At the beginning of the relationship, it's easier to do that with little overtures than with big ones.

## The First "Moment of Truth"

Some people think the "moment of truth" in the sale is the point at which the pen comes out and the person's name gets written down on the agreement. Actually, our *initial* point of contact in the conversation – the point at which the other person *starts* reciprocating our interest and interacting with us – is the first "moment of truth." What comes out at the end of the process may well be a huge sale, and we may well earn a massive commission on it ... but the true Sales Master *earns* that commission by what he or she does long before the pen touches the paper.

So we don't ask for everything up front, and we certainly don't try to get a major commitment before we've built up any meaningful relationship with the other person. We take baby steps. In fact, we never even *try* to "close a big deal." *We focus instead on securing one small commitment at a time.*

## A Mexican adventure

Here's a true story about something that happened to me in Mexico. My daughter Morgan and I were on vacation there one July; we had been walking for hours, and it was incredibly hot out. We were dragging.

After a long day exploring, we made our way down a little, sweltering city street together, exhausted and overcooked. There we saw a small jewelry store. In the window of the store was a remarkable thing: a sign that read *Aire Acondicionado*.

The sign was written in huge blue script with icicles hanging down from each letter. At that moment, it was the most beautiful thing we had ever seen.

We stepped into the store, which was, as advertised, cool and serene. Instant relief! The lady behind the counter greeted us with "Buenos días!" and a big, broad smile.

### Baby step!

As you might imagine, we weren't in any particular hurry to get back out into that hundred-degree-plus weather. So we browsed the cabinets in the store, looking at the merchandise. After a few minutes, Morgan paused thoughtfully over a striking natural stone necklace. Quietly, the store owner glided out from behind the counter and made her way next to Morgan. She said, "Beautiful, *sí?*"

### Baby step!

Morgan agreed that the necklace was beautiful. The store owner said, "Let me take it out." I was not particularly enthusiastic about this, but Morgan thought it was a pretty good idea. Her face lit up when the necklace came out of the display case.

### Baby step!

By this time, I was over with Morgan, looking at the necklace, too. The store owner said, "Put it on!" I was uneasy about this, but the store owner smiled broadly again and said, "*Señor!* It's just for fun!" We laughed at that, and Morgan put the necklace on. I had to admit that it looked pretty good on her.

### Baby step!

Then the store owner said, "Want to see what it looks like on Mexican TV?" We were a little puzzled by this question. Then the owner led us over to a large mirror. As we stood and looked into it, we were still a little puzzled about what "Mexican TV" was. Then we looked at each other and got it – the "TV" was the mirror. (See how the store owner used self-deprecating humor to loosen things up?). We laughed, enjoying the absurd moment – and then Morgan took a long look at herself wearing the necklace. She liked what she saw.

### Baby step!

The whole time Morgan was admiring herself on "Mexican TV," the store owner was smiling and pleasant. We were going to buy, and she knew it. She had been "closing" us long before we walked in the door! In fact, when did the "closing" process actually begin?

When we saw the sign telling us about the jewelry store's air conditioning!

## One step at a time

Look at what happened there. She helped us to sell *ourselves* on that necklace. She didn't ram anything down our throat. She was just having fun! (And she was, too, all the way through the whole process, which she clearly knew like the back of her hand.)

Sometimes we forget about baby steps. Sometimes we want to walk in huge strides, to take "one giant leap for mankind" ... and we want to act like we've got a major commitment when we really don't have anything yet.

She saw us buying ... but all she *said* was, "Beautiful, *sí?*"

## You already know how to do this

Believe it! You really do know how to take "Baby Steps" to close the deal.

Can you think of ONE time in your life when you knew, instinctively, that it would have been a mistake to ask someone for too much, too early in the relationship – a time when you eventually got what you were after?

Yes _____
No _____

If yes, who was that person?

_____

What ultimately happened?

_____

# Skill 8

## Keep Your Eyes on the Prize

### Principle #8: Relish the Word "No"

*""If I work on a certain move constantly, then finally, it doesn't seem risky to me. The idea is that the move stays dangerous and it looks dangerous to my foes, but it is not to me. Hard work has made it easy."*

– Nadia Comăneci, five-time Olympic gold medalist

Nadia Comăneci may not have realized it, but what she was really talking about when she described working "on a certain move constantly" was positive internal visualization in the face of setbacks during the selling cycle.

She was talking about the power of *routine*.

Make no mistake: our routine really is something we control, something that connects directly to our level of sales achievement. Routine in the face of seemingly "dangerous" situations has everything to do with the way we allow ourselves to process (so-called) "rejection." Hard work can make handling these "dangerous" situations easy. But the work must happen within us. We must teach ourselves to focus automatically on the goal ahead of us, and not on the bump in the road along the way. We must teach ourselves to keep our *eyes on the prize.*

If we build, and *practice*, a routine of positive internal response when we come up against (apparent) rejection – ("This is no big deal; I've gotten business from someone who said that before; this is a relationship where I can add value") – we'll learn to keep our eyes on the prize as a matter of course. And turnarounds that might seem impossible to others will become second nature to us.

We have to practice *seeing our goal already achieved* when we hear "No." Whenever we hear "No" with our ears, we have to see, in our mind's eye, the prize we are striving for! Then and only then can we respond effectively to what the person just said. We have to practice, and take full control of, our own *emotional and mental responses* when we hear "No."

Our own *habits of mind* are what determine whether or not we are "rejected" in any real sense of that word.

If you think r*outinely*, repeatedly, and with power and precision, about exactly what you're bringing into reality in your life … if you do that until that routine yields a *white heat of concentration and focus* … if you keep your *eyes on the prize* … you will find it becomes easy to remain poised in the face of the word "No."

You must, of course, know exactly what your goal *is*, and you must fully experience the reality of it within your mind, if you truly wish to stare down the word "No" – and *Close and Grow Rich.* If you can do that, you will literally come to look forward to the word "No" from your prospects – and you will find that seeming "rejection" will actually energize you and renew your commitment!

## Authority

Don't make the mistake of thinking that the minute a prospect throws the word "No" on the table, you have lost authority in the conversation. Actually, all that's happened is you've gotten a chance to show the prospect *who you really are.* This is what you do for a living! You keep your eyes on the prize when people say "No!"

Am I saying that you should continue to try to ram the same exact idea down someone's throat, over and over again, even after you hear them tell you that they can't find any possible way to make it work? No. Don't browbeat the person; don't ask the same question seven times in a row. That's not what I'm talking about here. I'm talking about keeping your eyes on the prize: staying focused, staying authentic, and staying *connected* to your prospect in the short term, the mid-term, and the long term ... without losing sight of what you're focused on bringing into reality in your life and the prospect's life. Even if no relationship emerges right now, what will happen tomorrow?

Does "No" really mean that there's no possibility of business from this person, ever? If you stop and think about all the people who ever bought from you or your organization ... and then calculate how many of them initially told you that they *couldn't* buy ... you'll understand what I'm talking about.

"No" is simply an opportunity for you to demonstrate what you're really focused on. If you hear "No," and you then simply shrug your shoulders and concede defeat, without making any attempt to follow through and enrich the relationship, you send one kind of message to the prospect. If you stand your ground, poke and prod a little bit, and figure out what the dimensions of this "No" really are … then find *some* way to add value to this person's world … then your selling style is more in line with the Sales Masters I've worked with over the years.

The word "No" should never keep you from identifying when and how it makes the most sense to continue the conversation.

## Getting "No" to work in your favor

Believe it or not, the word "No" is a very powerful force that can actually work in your favor as the sales process plays out.

Dr. Robert Cialdini, author of *Influence: The Psychology of Persuasion*, has done some amazing work in this area. His research indicates that when prospects say "No," to one thing, their likelihood of saying "Yes" to something else increases with the next exchange.

People really do want to give you some point of agreeability. The real Sales Masters understand that they have to get a few "No's" out of the way so they can earn the "Yes" answers at the most critical time. The trick is doing this in such a way that we get the dialogue to *continue*, not stop in its tracks when you run into a temporary setback. To keep that dialogue going, keep your eyes on the prize – the mutually beneficial relationship you can deliver!

So don't try to convince – inspire! Keep your footing! Stay connected! Many prospects will use the word "No" to test your mettle. Send them the right message – that you know what your *real* job is. Your *real* job is to keep your eyes on the prize – and avoid being "spooked" by the word "No."

## Authentic responses to "No"

Here are some real-life exchanges based on actual encounters some Sales Masters I've worked with have had with prospects who initially said "No." (The details have been changed to protect the innocent.) Obviously, these exchanges happened *after* the Sales Master in question had established commonality and rapport, and *after* he or she had gotten the other person to open up about what was actually happening in their world.

**Tactic 1:**

*Prospect:* "Our budget is spent for this year."

*Sales Master Susan:* "Okay. Let me ask you this: If the budget wasn't full this year – are you saying you would work with us?"

*Prospect:* "Sure, if I had the money, I'd like to."

*Sales Master Susan:* "Well – how about we go ahead and get started, and we invoice you in the second quarter of next year?"

(She got that deal.)

**Tactic 2:**

*Prospect:* "You know what? I looked your proposal over – I

don't think you've got enough experience in our industry."

*Sales Master Chuck:* "Wow – the only thing I can say is, what could I have left out? Because quite frankly, in our areas of expertise, we really are the most experienced in this industry. Is there something more you're looking for? If I can't do it, maybe I can point you toward someone else who can."

*Prospect:* "Well, we want A, B, and C. I guess I didn't share that with you earlier."

*Sales Master Chuck:* "Aha – well, I should have asked. Can I just share something with you? Our company does do A, B, and C – but I realize I may not have explored that with you before. Let's take a couple of minutes to go over this right now."

(He knew the objective was to keep the dialogue going. He got that deal.)

**Tactic 3:**

*Prospect:* "You know, I've got to be honest with you – just got a call from my CEO, he's pulled the plug on this thing, and he wants his brother-in-law to do it."

*Sales Master Ashley:* "Well, nobody wants to compete with the brother-in-law. I have to tell you, though: The last time I did business with my brother-in-law it turned out to be one of the most miserable decisions I ever made. I've always had a belief that mixing money and family is like mixing oil and water. Don't get me wrong. I think brothers-in-law are great for dinner parties, and great for coming over and going fishing. But when you start mixing business with family, it just never seems to work out. Now, then – that's just one person's opinion, and obviously I really want your business. Would you be willing to reconsider, and build a bridge to somebody who can give you an arm's-length-transaction? And by the way, do you know what the power of an arm's-length transaction is? If I screw up, if I don't deliver, you can come down on me. If the CEO's brother-in-law screws up, you can't. He doesn't have to look at me across the Christmas dinner table. If I could get you a 'brother-in-law' price on this, and throw in A, B, and C, would you consider going with us to the CEO's office?"

(She got that deal.)

**Tactic 4:**

*Prospect:* "Do me a favor and call me next quarter. This looks interesting. Let's talk in March."

*Sales Master Gene:* "Can I ask you something?"

*Prospect:* "Sure."

*Sales Master Gene:* "What's going to be different in March from what we're looking at right now? (No answer.) Let's look at this. You need this now, and in March, you'll be in worse shape than you are now, and the price will probably have gone up by then. So why would you wait until you need it more and have to spend more to get it?"

(He got that deal.)

## She thanked him!

One Sales Master I know told me of a time when, during a single presentation, the prospect said "No" *six separate times.* Each time, this Sales Master kept his eyes on the prize, changed course, thought of a new twist, offered a new benefit, and *kept going.* At the end of the presentation, the prospect not only agreed to give him the business ... but thanked him for not giving in when she tried to reject him!

When I share these kinds of stories with people at my seminars, they sometimes give a little nervous laugh and say something like, "Yeah, but those people are special. *I* can't do that."

And that's when I unleash my secret weapon: Nadia Comăneci.

I say, "Guys – why do you think those Sales Masters *can* do that? Because they're confident in what they're doing. And *why* are they confident in what they're doing? Because they have a routine. Just like Nadia Comăneci. They practice *what they're going to see, hear, and feel internally* when they hear someone say 'No.' They practice that over and over and over again. It *looks* dangerous – but it's not really, *because they practice all the time.*"

# You already know how to do this

Believe it! You really do know how to "Keep Your Eyes on the Prize."

Can you think of ONE time in your life when you were able to focus more powerfully on what you were moving *toward* than on what seemed to stand in the way?

Yes  _____
No  _____

If yes, what was your goal?

_____

What obstacles did you face?

_____

What ultimately happened?

_____

# Skill 9

## Crack the Code

### Principle #9: Organization Means Knowing Your Process and Knowing Your Prospect

*"When I accepted the commission (to create a piece of sculpture for CIA headquarters), I had something of an epiphany in the research I did about the agency, actually the science of espionage. I realized there is a connection between the sciences and the invisible forces of man."*

– James Sanborn, American sculptor

T rue story: James Sanborn was commissioned to create a one-of-a-kind piece of artwork known as *Kryptos* for a one-of-a-kind client: the CIA.

Sanborn's quote (above) is instructive. In order to create the work, he himself had to become a code-breaker, and was trained by elite CIA staff in this great art. The sculpture he placed in front of the Central Intelligence Agency's Langley, Virginia headquarters was a puzzle ... a code to be cracked. Installed in 1999, it has yet to yield its full secret to the world.

Writing about the sculpture shortly after it was installed, the *Washington Post* commented: "(Sanborn's) work often deals with mystery and the hidden forces of nature, (and he) jumped at the chance to do a sculpture for the intelligence agency. He proposed an artwork that contained its own puzzle, and the agency quickly agreed. He said he was contacted repeatedly by amateur code-breakers hoping for advice, a clue, anything. 'About every couple of months, sometimes more, somebody would call me up...I had nothing whatsoever to do with any of these people,' he said with disdain. 'It's about the thrill of discovery.'"

When we deal with our customers, most of us act just like those amateur code-breakers who appear out of nowhere, and demand, with no particularly good reason, to receive a "hint" about the puzzle's solution. Should we really be surprised when the person we want to sell to opts out of the relationship and thereafter has "nothing to do" with us? Should we really be surprised when the prospect expects us to embrace the "thrill of discovery" ... and do a little exploring on our own?

## The thrill of discovery: Two arenas

Just as a master spy must do "research" and truly understand the science of what he does for a living, you, too, must do *your* research and understand the science behind what *you* do for a living. In pursuing these goals, you should think of yourself as a sleuth, as someone who is out to "crack the code" on two important fronts – the first being *your own sales process*, and the second being any given prospect or customer's *unique situation*. Both of these intelligence areas are essential areas of mastery for anyone who wishes to *Close and Grow Rich*.

## Cracking the code: Your own sales process

If they want to live for very long, spies have to be organized.

Salespeople who thrive have to be organized, too. But most salespeople misunderstand what I mean when they hear me say that. They think I mean that I want them to use a particular filing system, or enter everything they do into a Blackberry, or change what happens on a piece of paper connected to their daily routine in a way that will make a sales manager happy. That's not the kind of organization I'm talking about at all.

The kind of organization I'm talking about has more to do with *knowing exactly what your own sales process looks like, and knowing where you are in it.* You identify your own process; you must know when someone is getting ready to buy and when someone isn't.

Organization, for salespeople, is a matter of knowing where you are and what has to happen next. If you don't know what has to happen next for the person to move from one stage of the

buying process to the next, *you have not yet cracked your own code.*
Consider these three categories.

### Prospect > "Hotspect" > Buyer

No matter what you sell, where you sell it, or how you sell it,
you may rest assured that the people you sell to go through the
three stages in the box above. A *prospect* is someone who is talking to you about buying. A *"hotspect"* is someone whose actions
*demonstrate* that he is statistically likely to buy from you. And a
*buyer* is someone who already has bought from you, and might
buy again.

Simple enough! In fact, this model applies to every salesperson
on earth.

Organization, for you, means knowing exactly what each of
those three stages look like *in your selling world,* and where you are
at any given moment in relation to them.

So: You're organized when you know whether the relationship
is really moving forward. You're organized when you can sense
what's truly important to the other person right now. You're organized to the extent that you can use *pronesia* to figure out what's
*about* to be important to the other person once you've learned
what's *been* important in the past. You're organized when you are
certain you're doing everything that needs to be done to help the
other person move from one stage to the next, without lingering
too long in one place.

I believe that most salespeople are disorganized – in the sense
I'm using the word "organization" here. The minority of salespeople, the true Sales Masters, while they sometimes may not

look as organized as some other people in certain areas of their life, are extremely organized in their sales process. I've seen some salespeople whom you might actually call scatterbrained people – you wonder how they get along. But the moment they get in front of a buyer, they have all their faculties organized.

## Cracking the code: This particular person

Spies crack codes and get intelligence. Throughout military history, this has been the obsession – how we can use our people to figure out what the other side is doing, how they're doing it, and what it all means. As a salesperson, you have a very similar mission.

On the one hand, this person you're talking to is utterly unique. On the other hand, you probably know a heck of a lot more about how people *typically* end up buying your product or service than this prospect does. "Cracking the code" of an individual thus means identifying what's unique about this person ... and how those unique elements might match up with your own sales process.

The process of matching those two halves up might take minutes, days, weeks, or months – but it is likely to begin with a question like "Tell me about what you personally are trying to get done here." If you don't understand this person's goal, then you are not organized, no matter how sharp your briefcase looks or how neat your handwriting is!

"Cracking the code" means embracing the thrill of discovery. It means understanding exactly who *this* prospect is ... identifying what *this* prospect is invested in and trying to make happen ... and once you've done that, sharing all the relevant "intelligence" on your side, the experience you and your organization have in areas that seem most similar to what the prospect is facing right now. If you do that effectively, you'll get a straight answer when you ask about buying criteria and about what the person has done before in your area of expertise. You'll get a straight answer when you ask what has worked and what hasn't. And you'll even get a straight answer when you ask what "the other guys" are doing in this account.

When you "crack the code," you understand what is actually happening in your prospect's world, and you don't run into sudden, mysterious obstacles like "this doesn't seem right" or "your price is too high" halfway through the buying process.

Become a sleuth! Keep a dossier! Use all the assets at your disposal! Use the processes I've given you in this book. Share something from your side – stop talking – and then learn something about this person's world. Then start connecting the dots. *Harness the "thrill of discovery" – and track down the intelligence you need to close the deal!*

## Know your process, know their process

How much do you really know about your selling process? How well do you understand your customer's buying process? You don't want to operate in the dark on either front.

Fortunately, all the answers are sitting right there in front of you. But you have to dig. Once you "crack the code," I think you'll be astonished at how easy decoding the message can be.

To the uninitiated, of course, decoding something as complex as, say, Morse code looks like something very close to impossible. So the task may look daunting at first. But once you figure out the system and grasp what the various dots and dashes mean, understanding the seemingly "hidden" message can actually become a matter of instinct.

Here's an example of what I mean: British code-breakers during World War II got so good at surreptitiously monitoring German telegraph communications that they could not only tell what the message was – they could tell, from the style of the man on the sending end, *which German telegraph operator was clicking the machine on the other end!* You really can get that good at figuring out the prospect/"hotspect"/buyer sequence in your world ... and at figuring out your prospect's actual buying processes.

## You already know how to do this

Believe it! You really do know how to "Crack the Code."

Was there ever a time when you had a task, puzzle, or research question to solve – one that involved getting information from someone you didn't know very well?

Yes \_\_\_\_
No \_\_\_\_

If yes, what was your goal?

_____

What obstacles did you face?

_____

What ultimately happened?

_____

Before you move on to the next chapter, ponder this question: *How did you feel when you finally cracked the code?*

## CLOSE AND GROW RICH

# Skill 10

## Clear the Decks

## Principle #10: One Thing At a Time

*"Most people have no idea of the giant capacity we can immediately command when we focus all of our resources on mastering a single area of our lives."*
– Anthony Robbins, Best-selling author of *Awaken the Giant Within*

The greatest thinkers, sages, saints, and poets of human history have disagreed on many, many points, but they have agreed on one: *We become what we think about ... if we think about that thing exclusively.*

It follows that one hundred percent of your attention is quite sufficient to transform your world and "magnetize" it toward what

Napoleon Hill referred to as your "definite chief aim in life." But there's a catch. Although 100% of your attention will in fact bring about this seeming miracle, *90%* of your attention definitely won't get you there – and in fact, 90% may put your gears into reverse!

At any given moment, you only have so much attention to give. And *shifting* your attention from one thing to another *reduces* the total amount of attention you have at your disposal, with adverse affects for you as a person.

This is not idle speculation, philosophical improvisation, or poetic license. It is, instead, a matter of confirmed science.

## Science chimes in

True story: A 2004 John Hopkins study concluded as follows:

"The evidence we have right now strongly suggests that attention is strictly limited – a zero-sum game. When attention is deployed to one modality ... it necessarily extracts a cost on another modality." The Johns Hopkins researchers discovered that "when a person was instructed to move his attention (to listen to something) ... the brain's parietal cortex and the prefrontal cortex produced a burst of activity that the researchers interpreted as a signal to initiate the shift of attention. This surprised them, because it has previously been thought that those parts of the brain were involved only in visual functions."

Translation: "Multi-tasking" always means you're short-changing *something*. And it's easier than we think to "multi-task" your way out of commitment to your "definite chief aim in life." This happens with astonishing ease during a meeting or conversation, or even during private time that we think we've devoted to a single activity.

As a Sales Master, you must never, ever short-change yourself. Keep in mind that your prospect, your financial goal, and your career, all interconnect. When you are working on one of these things, you must be working on it and it alone, and you must devote all of your attention to it. The act of committing all of your consciousness to a given, carefully chosen target is not just a "sometime" thing – it is a necessary moment-to-moment habit for all who wish to *Close and Grow Rich*.

## Learn to Focus Without Distraction

"Clearing the decks" means focusing with absolutely undivided attention on what's in front of you, moment by moment by moment. To make this method of interacting with the world your habit, not just your catch-phrase, you are well advised to adopt a simple, one-sentence motto. You could do worse than to repeat this motto to yourself, out loud, upon arising each morning:

**One thing, and only one thing, at a time.**

If you're in a meeting with a prospect, it follows from this principle that you should be focusing with complete, rapt attention on the prospect.

So before you even step into that meeting, you must resolve to rid yourself of every possible distraction: how you feel about your husband or wife at the moment, whether you like your job, whether you're ahead of quota or behind quota, whether your mom was good to you while you were young – *everything* except the other person you're about to connect with. For the purposes of this meeting, *he or she is all that exists*. If you're not doing that, you're not yet clearing the decks!

Similarly, if you're working on a proposal, you should be *only* working on a proposal … not answering e-mail at the same time.

If you're asking questions and uncovering information, you should be *only* asking questions and uncovering information … not making your formal presentation.

No multi-tasking!

The kind of profoundly focused attention I'm talking about definitely takes practice, and perhaps a little soul-searching, to summon. (See my book *What's Your Sales DNA?* for a fuller discussion of the soul-searching half of this equation.)

Whatever effort must take place to instill this habit, however, *is worth it.* This extraordinary level of focus is a necessary precondition of the divine gift we have identified earlier in this book as "empathic intelligence" – the ability to identify what another person is likely to consider important. In fact, I believe that God gave us two ears and one mouth for a reason—so that salespeople would remember the proper ratio of speaking to hearing in the sales process!

In a sales setting, we should all be listening at least two-thirds of the time and talking (at most) one-third of the time with our prospects. But for some reason, most salespeople manage to flip it around the other direction and talk two-thirds of the time and listen one-third of the time (or even less). *They are multi-tasking!* As the prospect is talking, guess what most salespeople are focused on? *What they're going to say next.* That means they do not truly hear what the other person is saying *right now.*

Sales Masters, on the other hand, are hooked in visually and aurally to their prospects, with total attention. They understand that we human beings listen with our eyes first and our ears second. (And by the way, the scientists agree on that point, as well.) If you're not "listening" to the person with your eyes first, then you simply won't be able to engage your ears in the act of connecting to this person, and you will turn the other person off. All you'll be doing is imitating what most salespeople do, which is sit there with the "lights on – but nobody home."

*Forget* about what you're going to say next! Pay absolutely undivided attention *to the person in front of you*, as though your success depended on him or her! (It does!) If you watch the person with total commitment and attention, then you will find that really you can "hear" what they're saying with your eyes, not with your ears.

By the way, visual attention is incredibly important for another reason: The body language you pick up on will often tell a story that's completely different than the "surface meaning" of the words you are hearing. Focusing on the customer with your *eyes first* allows you to truly garner what the total message is. It is definitely *not* just a transcript of the words that are coming out of your prospect's mouth. (If the words themselves were all that you needed, we would all be closing our sales via e-mail … but somehow that never seems to happen, does it?)

Today, try an experiment. Try, just for today, to live the whole day "one minute at a time" …. by vowing to "listen" to everyone you meet with your eyes first, and your ears second.

## Minute by minute

I've emphasized this critical "one thing at a time" principle here in its most obvious application – as it relates to your direct, face-to-face interactions with prospects. But once you implement the idea in that setting, you will quickly realize that the "one thing at a time" rule is actually directly relevant to *every single minute of your selling day.* Your planning for the next day, for instance, deserves 100% of your attention. Don't multi-task as you sell or plan to sell – even though everyone else on earth seems to be trying to do this. Focus without compromise or distraction on your stated goal, whatever it is, for the next, say, fifteen minutes. Then move on to what you plan to accomplish in the *next* fifteen minutes, devoting your full attention to *that* and that alone.

Yes, this takes discipline and the effort that always accompanies a change of habit. Yes, you can be a "good" salesperson without learning to focus your attention – and your day – like a proverbial laser-beam. But did you pick up this book to become *good* … or to become *great* at what you do?

# You already know how to do this

Believe it! You really do know how to "Clear the Decks."

Was there ever a time when you "won someone over" by paying very, very close attention to him or her?

Yes ____
No ____

If yes, who was the person?

_____

How did he or she know that you were fully committed to improving the relationship?

_____

What ultimately happened?

_____

Before you move on to the next chapter, ponder this question: *What distractions did you have to tune out in order to pay attention to the person at that level?*

# Intermission

## Getting Ready
## for the Master Class

U p to this point, you have reawakened ten skills capable of transforming your career and turning you into a Master Closer. Look at them once again:

Skill #1: Finding Mastery

Skill #2: Using the Law of Commonality

Skill #3: Getting Serious by Lightening Up

Skill #4: Unlock the Intuitive Power of People-Reading

Skill #5: Establish an Unfair Advantage

Skill #6: Use the Velvet Hammer

Skill #7: Take Baby Steps

Skill #8: Keep Your Eyes on the Prize

Skill #9: Crack the Code

Skill #10: Clear the Decks

That's a lot of ground for anyone to cover, and I realize that most authors composing a book on this topic would probably be content to cover *only* those principles. That's because most *salespeople* would be content for the book to cover only those ten ideas. *And yet ... most salespeople wouldn't even have made it this far in the book. You did.*

## The master class

We now enter the "master class." In this latter part of the book – namely, Skills number Eleven, Twelve, Thirteen, and Fourteen – I want to show you what "saving the best for last" really means. I've created a master class for you, because by making it this far in the book, you've *demonstrated* that you have a commitment to Mastery. If you're still with me here in Skill Number Eleven, you've proven that you're willing to take your game to the next level.

Think of it this way: Once you master the ten skills we've covered thus far, once you implement them on a consistent basis, you will be like the student who works for a period of years to attain the coveted *black belt* in a martial arts discipline like karate. What will you do then?

Don't misunderstand: a black belt is wonderful ... but what *kind* of black belt are we talking about?

Do you remember what we learned together in the first part of this book? There are different levels of mastery, and *the black belt is the beginning of a process, not the end of one.* There's a first-degree black belt, a second-degree black belt, a third-degree black belt, and so on.

Sure. You *could* stop here. You could master the ten basic principles ... and that would be really good. But did you start this book to be good ... or to become as *great* as you can possibly be at the art of closing?

I thought that's what you'd say. Let's keep going!

# Skill 11

## Biggie-Size Your Commissions ... by Downselling

### Principle #11: Move up by moving down.

*"All credibility, all good conscience, and all evidence of truth come only from our sensory interactions with others."*
– Friedrich Nietzsche, German philosopher

Throughout this book, we've been talking about how you, as a salesperson, interact with prospects. Now let's turn the tables for a moment. Say *you're* the one in an appliance store, examining merchandise. How do *you* react when a salesperson approaches *you* on and says something brilliant like, "Can I help you?"

If you're like most of us, you shut down. You close the window of communication tight by saying something like, "No, thanks.

I'm just looking." There's no chance for your mind to connect with the salesperson's for even an instant. No rapport or commonality is likely between you and the salesperson in the immediate future.

Now rewind the tape and start over. Suppose the salesperson takes a different approach.

Suppose that, as you're looking at, say, a fancy refrigerator, the salesperson walks up to you and says, "Hi, I'm Joan – welcome to Grady's Department Store. That's our high-end model, and it's a beautiful refrigerator, but just between you and me, I think it's a little overpriced. You can get exactly the same features, and just a little less chrome, on the H-4100 unit, which is right over here – and it costs $200 less. Just thought you might want to know. Can I ask what brings you into the store today?"

Wow! What a difference!

Does the communication window shut tight at *that* moment? Probably not.

Is there a chance for your mind to connect with that salesperson's? Absolutely.

Is there the possibility of rapport-building and commonality? Sure. This person seems eager to identify the best possible value, just like you are. In fact, even if you aren't really in the market for a refrigerator right now, you might start to think about what else this salesperson might be able to tell you about other products. When you think about that high-definition television set, which is what you're *really* thinking about buying, you immediately start wondering what *other* information this person could share with you.

Is there at least the possibility of discussion about a purchase in your immediate future? You bet there is.

So what happened?

I'll tell you what happened. The salesperson *gave something first ... by downselling you.* He built up credibility and made an investment in the relationship by sharing some of his knowledge in a way that gave you a potential advantage. He made it clear that he wasn't trying to shove the highest-priced model in the store down your throat.

By giving you something first, that salesperson was shaping your perceptions. Not about the refrigerator, necessarily ... he was shaping your perceptions about *him.*

## The law of reciprocation

When we downsell like this, we actually "biggie-size" our commissions. We move up (in the relationship) by moving down (in the price). And we take advantage of the *Law of Reciprocation*, which is a critical closing principle. Take a look:

When we take the initiative and create value for others first, they feel an obligation to respond in kind.

We create the value by downselling rather than upselling; they feel an obligation to respond with something in return, like a discussion about their buying priorities. *And that's really what we want, isn't it?*

Now, creating value where it did not exist before is not simply a matter of blurting out the words, "That model over there is $200 cheaper," then walking away. Creating value means taking the initiative and visualizing that value, actually experiencing it for the other person, and growing the relationship from there. It's a matter of planting a seed in the other person's mind. Ultimately, it's a matter of faith. *If you think about this person as though you have already delivered value for him or her, and act accordingly, value will come back to you.*

## Downselling in Action

Bill worked at a company that sold, among other things, high-end stereo systems; some of them were quite expensive. People would walk into Bill's showroom and gaze longingly at the top-of-the-line model, which was quite spectacular. He'd always start his discussions by saying this: "That's a beautiful system, but the price puts a lot of people off."

What a great opening!

The customer would say something like, "Yeah? How much is it?"

Bill would say, "It's $5500..." (And here he would wait for the customer to show some kind of body language that indicated discomfort about paying that much money; if that's what happened, he would continue with ...) "But you know what? You could spend a lot less and still get a great system. Here – let me show you my favorite ..."

And he was off to the races. He would start at $3500 and work his way *down* to $1900. Of course, that stands in stark contrast to what most salespeople would do in that situation, which is start at, say, the $1000 level and try, in vain, to work their way *up*. That's known as "lowballing," and it's not what Sales Masters do. (They're too busy envisioning the handshake that seals a high-end sale!)

The truly beautiful part about Bill's approach is, a certain percentage of the people he approaches will *upsell themselves.* They'll say, "Actually, $5500 isn't that bad ... it's at the upper end of my range, but it's in my range. Tell me more about this system." Now, that's an outcome lowballing will simply never deliver for you!

If you were to ask Bill what his "best conversation" with a prospect sounds like, he might well recall an exchange like this:

*Sales Master Bill: I was going to show you this system, but I think it's not quite right for you.*

*Prospect: Why do you say that?*

*Sales Master: Well, it's a little pricey.*

*Prospect: Let me take a look at it.*

Bingo! Bill has just biggie-sized his commission ... by downselling.

The prospect will always bond better with a salesperson who says, "You could spend a lot less." Downselling makes it easy for people to *volunteer* to give you the order!

## More Downselling in Action

Sometimes, in new home sales, on-site agents are faced with the challenge of having to sell a home that's not as desirable as some of the others in the same neighborhood. For instance, the view isn't that great, because the property is backed up against a power line. Downselling is an absolutely perfect selling principle for these situations.

The homeowner tours the property and says something like, "Well, I like the floor layout, and the southern exposure is what I'm looking for, but the view out the back window isn't great."

You know what Sales Masters say?

"Actually, that's *exactly* why I brought you here. You're saving $30,000 on this home, and it seemed to me like it matched up with the price range you and I were kicking around. And I wanted to tell you what Jack, the guy who lives next door, concluded about that view. He said, 'I think what I'm going to do is take the $30,000 I'm saving and decorate the house with it!' He said, 'My wife was ecstatic. She's just going to throw up a big curtain against that back wall.' For Jack, the view was the reason to get in."

The beautiful thing about this discussion is that the buyer who wants a bargain will listen to your logic. You're painting a picture for him of how he can get into the community without going out of his price bracket. You're planting the seed of an idea and watering it.

What about the buyer who *doesn't* see this price break as a great advantage? Guess what? He's making a buying statement ... and *upselling himself!*

You can guess what the Sales Masters say in that situation: "No problem – let's go take a look at another home!"

## Still More Downselling in Action

Suzy worked as the office manager in a small real estate office. After a discussion with her boss about how important it is to improve the visual appeal of the documents that go out of the office, Suzy received authorization to spend up to $400 on a quality color printer. She called up a local office equipment dealer, and Jill, one of the salespeople for a major manufacturer, showed up for an appointment.

She looked at the models in the salesperson's brochure, and

found one that cost about $400. She asked Jill about that printer, and heard this in response:

"Actually, that model has a lot of fancy chrome on the outside, but it has virtually the same page-per-minute capacity, and the same color output, as this other model, the BYT-3030 ... and it's seventy-five dollars less."

Naturally, Suzy was a little curious about why the second unit cost seventy-five dollars less. She found out that it was because the unit was part of a special promotion the manufacturer was offering; there was no quality difference whatsoever between the two machines.

On the spot, Suzy issued a purchase order for the BYT-3030. She felt great; she had just saved her company seventy-five bucks, and she had found a salesperson she trusted.

Near the end of the meeting, Suzy asked Jill if her company handled copiers as well. (Recently, her boss had asked her to get a quote on a new copy machine.) As it turned out, Jill's company *did* represent a major copier company. The two scheduled another meeting, and 30 days later, Suzy took delivery on a $2000 copier.

What made that sale possible? You guessed it: Jill's willingness to downsell. That's what built up the trust that made the later $2000 sale possible.

## You already know how to do this

Believe it! You really do know how to "Downsell."

Was there ever a time when you made an "insider recommendation" that genuinely benefited the person you were talking to, and built credibility for you?

Yes _____
No _____

If yes, who was the person?

_____

How did the relationship change when you shared your recommendation?

_____

Before you move on to the next chapter, ponder this question: *How did looking out for the other person's interest end up advancing your interests?*

# Skill 12

## Harness the Power of Reasonable Doubt

### Principle #12: Never bash the other guys

*"I hate the man who builds his name /*
*On ruins of another's fame."*
– John Gay, English poet and dramatist

Let's start with the easy part: I never, ever use the word "competition" when I'm interacting with a prospect, and you shouldn't, either.

Saying the word "competition" out loud gives those folks an automatic promotion and raises them to my level, which is something that they don't deserve. So when I'm in discussion with a prospect, and the subject turns to the other people and companies the prospect could conceivably buy from, I never let that word "competition" escape my lips. What I call them is "the other guys." That's a much more accurate description of what we're talking about – someone who *isn't me* and *isn't working for my organization.* And by the way, when I use the phrase "the other guys," guess what happens? The prospect follows suit and starts calling them "the other guys," too, rather than "the competitors!"

That's the easy lesson. Now, for the hard lesson. You must never, ever bash the "other guys." And here's why.

## You can't afford the luxury of a putdown

There is simply no better way to kill a sale than to start a negative thought pattern within your own mind.

You cannot afford the luxury of a planned verbal attack on the "other guys." If you're getting ready for a meeting with someone who wants to talk about working with you, and you start using your mental resources to catalogue all the terrible things you can say about the "other guys," that makes it that much harder for you to see, hear, and experience your prospect *already using* your product or service and *benefiting* from what you have to offer. Instead, you're on the defensive. You're anxiously preparing for what you imagine will be an attack: the prospect may say that the "other guys" are offering better terms, better service, whatever. You're seeing negative outcomes because you're wiring your mind to experience all the wrong stuff: not what you *do* offer, but what the competition *doesn't.* And what you think about, you will bring about.

Here's the point. Don't fixate on the "other guys." Don't plan all kinds of responses to address what they may or may not be offering your prospect. Don't badmouth them. If you do, you'll definitely kill the "tingle," and you'll probably end up placing the prospect's attention on the very last people in the world you want him or her to think about. Just get back to your top story – namely, what *you* want to deliver to your prospect.

## "So what do I say?"

Am I saying you should pretend that the "other guys" don't exist? No.

You do have to respond intelligently if the *prospect* raises the issue of what the "other guys" are offering. But your goal is to do that in a way that keeps positive emotion from flickering out, *in your mind or the prospect's mind,* and allows you to return quickly to your "top story."

Here's the very best advice I can give you for doing that: *Raise a reasonable doubt, and then stop talking.*

Don't go into full "attack mode," and don't deliver long monologues or horror stories. Just come up with a single, memorable sentence that *implies* (but does not state outright) that working with the other guys *might* not be the smartest move. Let the prospect's imagination do the rest.

Johnnie Cochran, the attorney who successfully defended O. J. Simpson, is probably the best example from popular culture of a man who concisely and successfully raised reasonable doubt. The Simpson case seemed to go on forever, and the prosecution had a massive sea of quite detailed evidence on its side. Maybe that sea of evidence was a little *too* detailed. Today, most people remember only one sentence from that trial. Apparently, it was the same sentence that the jury remembered: *If the glove don't fit, you must acquit.*

Cochran gave the jury a memorable, compelling way of summing up the defense's position. He raised a reasonable doubt. And he won the case.

## Reasonable doubt in action

Here are some real-life strategies I've used, and trained Sales Masters to use, to raise reasonable doubt with prospects who wanted to talk about the "other guys."

**Example #1:**

*Prospect:* The other guys are charging $10,000 less than you are.

*Sales Master Jean:* Well, I would hope so.

(Jean didn't fill in the blanks – she gave a knowing glance, and then she shut up! The prospect tried to fill in the blanks: "What do you mean?" Jean declined the offer: – "I'm not going to say anything bad about them – but I will point out something that my daddy always told me: 'You get what you... what?' The prospect finished the sentence: "...pay for." Jean got back to talking about what they both were excited about. She closed the deal.)

**Example #3:**

*Prospect:* The other guys are offering X, Y, and Z if I go with them.

*Sales Master Ed:* Hmm ... I wonder why?

(Ed didn't fill in the blanks – he gave a knowing glance, and then he shut up! The prospect filled in the blanks ... and then they had a good discussion about how some things may look free, but really aren't. Ed never talked about the competition directly. He got back to talking about what he and the prospect were both excited about. He closed the deal.)

Get the idea? Don't ever sling mud, because you just lose the ground beneath yourself. Raise a reasonable doubt, and then stop talking for a minute. You'll find a way to get back to your main story. You know why? Because *when imagination comes into conflict with reality, imagination usually wins.*

## You already know how to do this

Believe it! You really do know how to "Avoid Bashing the Other Guys" and "Raise a Reasonable Doubt."

Were you ever able to "take the high road" and overcome a rival or competitor ... without ever actually speaking badly of that person?

Yes ___
No ___

What was the situation?

_____

What did you say?

_____

Before you move on to the next chapter, ponder this question: *What would have happened if you had not "taken the high road"?*

# Skill 13

## Use the Hypnotic Power of Cadence

### Principle #13: Don't change gears suddenly

*"Persuasion happens to be not a science, but an art."*
William Bernbach, legendary advertising executive

Don't get intimidated by the words "hypnotic" and "cadence" in this Skill. This chapter is about nothing more or less than the art of persuasion. In it, I hope to share a few principles that will, I believe, help you to master that art – even though I must caution you that mastering it is really the work of a lifetime. But every great artist starts somewhere, and every great work of art was once an idea. The idea you will find within this chapter can, I believe, elevate your sales "game" to a whole new level.

There is a critical point in any sales discussion where the "window" opens, when there is a mutual focus on a shared benefit, and when you, the salesperson, are perfectly positioned to close the transaction. The deal is simply waiting there for you. "Using the hypnotic power of cadence" simply means maintaining the same kind of rhythm, tonality, eye contact, and continuity that got you to that point.

It means supporting that precious moment – rather than interrupting it by introducing a new, *unfamiliar* rhythm … a jarringly *different* tonality … a sudden *lack* of eye contact … or a totally *unexpected* element that has not come up in the conversation before.

You're responsible for maintaining the good "ambience" of this conversation. You're responsible for the survival of the idea you've planted in the prospect's mind. And to do that, you must assume responsibility for the sequencing, rhythm, and cadence of the conversation – for the "beat," if you will.

To put another way: If you wish to become a true Sales Master, you and you alone are responsible for putting the principles of "Sales-nosis" to work in your sales cycle.

## Salesnosis

**Salesnosis: The art of hypnotic persuasion.**

Okay. So it's not *really* in Webster's Dictionary. But Salesnosis is an important concept; it is an art you can and should master. Before you get all worked up about the idea of "hypnotizing" prospects … before you start wondering whether I'm talking about getting prospects to make chicken noises on your command …

let me clarify things a little bit. Mastering Salesnosis simply means mastering this one undeniable principle:

## Rhythm and cadence matter.

What do those four words mean to you? It means we human beings are more affected by "beat," rhythm and cadence than we might sometimes like to admit.

Have you ever had this experience? You pull up in the driveway after a long day at work, put the car in park, sit there for a second, take in your surroundings, and begin to reach for the keys in the ignition. Before you do that, though, a strange realization crosses your mind: you have no memory whatsoever of the previous thirty minutes. The scary part is, you can't even remember the stop signs and red lights. You assume you must have noticed and obeyed them ... but you simply have no remembrance of doing so.

Would you like to know *why* you don't remember the drive home? Because you've become utterly familiar with the *rhythm* of the drive home. In fact, you've become so familiar with it, and you regard it as such a safe place, that you literally allow yourself to be lulled into a light trance as you're driving home. You were literally hypnotized!

Mildly hypnotized, perhaps, but hypnotized all the same. No, it was not a deep trance. It was a *light* trance – and you were in a *heightened* state of awareness as you experienced it. That's why you were able to navigate the red lights and stop signs successfully. And here we come to the truly interesting thing about this state of mind: you would have "snapped yourself out of it" *instantly* if you had perceived the slightest hint of danger.

Now: What would cause you to perceive danger while driving home? *A sudden change in your surroundings.* A break in the sequence you've become comfortable with. An alteration in the "beat." (Like, for instance, a deer staring into your headlights.)

Well, it's exactly the same with prospects. When they sense a change in the rhythm, in the beat, in the continuity, their "security alert" goes off. They tense up. They become wary. And wary people don't close deals.

Salespeople who understand and act on these basic principles of human mental functioning are, whether they know it or not, practicing Salesnosis.

## The art of influence

There really is a hypnotic element to the art of influence. No, we can't turn people into zombies, and we shouldn't want to. Unscrupulous manipulation of the unconscious is no more a part of the sales process than it is part of you driving home from work! What we're talking about is supporting the *comfort level* necessary to help the person make a decision that we honestly believe does benefit them.

If we change gears suddenly and unexpectedly by throwing a lot of brand-new elements at our prospects at the "moment of truth" … if we disrupt the rhythm they've grown used to … or if we suddenly stop looking them in the eye … they'll conclude, at an unconscious level, that something is wrong. And they'll be correct. Something *is* wrong. We're not supporting them as we have a responsibility to do.

As a result, they will shut down. Instantly. The window will close. The moment will pass. As professional salespeople, it's our duty, and our responsibility, to make sure that doesn't happen.

If you truly want the idea you've planted in the other person's mind to sprout, you must not trample it at the moment the buds appear! If you grasp this much, then you grasp the importance of cadence and rhythm in the selling process.

## Three possibilities

So picture this. You're face to face with a person who's interested in what you have to sell. You've established a good, solid interpersonal connection with the prospect, and you feel confident that you've reached the "moment of truth," the moment when you've earned the right to ask for the business. So, without breaking the rhythm you've established, you ask for the business, using a closing statement that you feel comfortable and authentic saying. It might sound like this:

> **"So – do you have any questions before we get the paperwork started?"**

Then what happens? I see three possibilities.

POSSIBILITY ONE: You might get a good, solid positive response from the prospect in return. ("No." And in this case, "no" truly does mean "yes"!) Congratulations! You've closed the deal.

POSSIBILITY TWO: On the other hand, you might get shot down. ("Whoa, wait a minute; I'm not ready to go forward with this yet.") Hmmm… maybe that wasn't the "moment of truth" after all. No problem. Just ask a question: "Okay – did I miss something? Usually, when we get to this point, people are pretty eager to move forward."

POSSIBILITY THREE: And then there's another possible reaction, one I call the Flinch.

You've seen the Flinch. In fact, you have almost certainly done it yourself when considering a major purchase. It's what happens when you purse your lips, knit your eyebrows together really tight, and quickly draw in air through your nose. Typically, after you do all these things in rapid succession, you'll say something like "Well, I don't know." (Try it now for yourself and you'll know exactly what I'm talking about: lips purse, eyebrows contract, air in through your nose, then say, "Well, I don't know." Got it? That's the Flinch.)

Here's what Sales Masters know that the rest of the selling world doesn't know: The Flinch indicates that the prospect is "on the fence." He or she could go either way. You can still move the sales process forward if you act authentically, instantly, and *without breaking the cadence of the conversation.*

In action, this close sounds like this.

*Sales Master Greg: So – do you have any questions before we get the paperwork started?*

*Prospect: (Purses lips, contracts eyebrows, draws air in rapidly through nose.)*

---

**Now: before the prospect can get the words "well, I don't know" out, you use this tiny gap as a slight pause in the conversation, and *without breaking the cadence,* you refocus on your "moment of truth" by appealing to a future benefit.**

---

*Sales Master Greg: Typically, people want to take a close look at Clause Nine, which has to do with the delivery date. I've penciled in January 1ˢᵗ because of what you were discussing earlier about shortening up your time to market. Does that date work for you?*

The phrase in italics, above, connects to the BENEFIT you are bringing to life. Is it a tangible reality that both you and the prospect can actually experience at this critical moment? If so, you're ready to roll.

You've probably heard the sales cliché: "He who speaks first loses." Actually, if you notice the Flinch quickly enough, if you are truly the *master* of the rhythm and sequence of your conversation, and if you know how to appeal confidently to the **benefit**, you have already brought into existence.

## Practice it!

Now, I am the first to admit that what I'm advocating here is not for amateurs. Rather, it is for people who have second-degree Black Belts in closing. It takes mastery of the rhythm of the conversation. It takes practice. It must be done with *total* (and I do mean total) confidence. But if you follow the steps I've just given you, you *will* turn around a large percentage of the Flinches that come your way.

## What most salespeople do

I placed this chapter about cadence here in the "master class" section of the book for a reason: What I'm telling you to do here is *very, very rare* in practice. Most salespeople (including me about twenty years ago) don't even know that cadence exists.

When the "moment of truth" comes, they freeze up, change their body language, change their tonality, or (even worse) stop the conversation in its tracks by saying things like this:

- "Let me go get the contract." (First of all, don't call it a contract – that's a scary word. Call it an agreement … that's friendlier. Second, you must have it with you at all times so you never, ever have to call a "time out" at the moment of truth. In fact, you should pull it out and appeal to it regularly throughout the sales process, so the prospect gets used to seeing it.)

- "Where's my pen? Let me go get one, hold on. I keep losing pens…" (Actually, you just lost the deal.)

- "Hey, let me show you something on the computer." (Which is, of course, not yet turned on. The dialogue skids to a halt as you wait for the computer to boot up.)

- "Let me go get you a brochure, it has a great picture of the widget we're talking about. Wait right here." (Why? So they can think twice about whether this is really a good idea – while you're rummaging around in the stockroom?)

Make sure, *ahead of time,* that everything you will need for this discussion is within easy reach. Don't change your body language. Don't change your vocal tonality. Don't suddenly start talking faster or slower than you were talking up to this point. *Don't break the cadence.*

## True story

When I'm interacting with prospects I plan to close, I always make sure to introduce a critical *prop* very early on in the face-to-face conversation – the pen.

I pull out a shiny, expensive pen as soon as possible, and I use that pen to sketch out ideas, diagrams, and even funny stories on any available writing surface. I use it as a pointer. I may even use it as a magic wand, if I get the chance to demonstrate one of my magic tricks to the prospect.

If you've been following this chapter closely, you know exactly why I use the pen in this way.

Of course! I want them to see that pen in action *throughout the conversation*, so that the pen doesn't come as a total surprise to them .... when I pull it out for them to use when signing the agreement.

That pen is their friend by this point. It's not something I pulled out of my pocket at the last minute. The sight of it is familiar; the clicking sound it makes when someone pushes the little button on top is familiar, too. If I establish what the pen is, what it looks like, and how it works, then it *doesn't break the cadence I've established* when the time is finally right for the prospect to *use* the pen ... and sign on the dotted line!

(Note: If you want to learn more about Salesnosis, just visit www.salesnosis.com.)

## You already know how to do this

Believe it! You really do know how to "Use the Hypnotic Power of Cadence."

Have you ever avoided putting some new issue on the table with someone who was important to you ... because you knew doing so would destroy the "moment"?

Yes _____
No _____

What happen?

_____

Before you move on to the next chapter, ponder this question: *How did you know that it would have been a mistake to disrupt the "ambience" in this way?*

# Skill 14

## Carpe Closum

### Principle #14: Watch the Bell Curve

*"Andy ... I'm a trained noticer. I notice these things."*
– Don Knotts, as Barney Fife, to Andy Griffith,
as Sheriff Andy Taylor, on *The Andy Griffith Show*

You've no doubt heard the Latin expression *carpe diem* – "seize the day." In the world of the Sales Master, the expression is rendered somewhat differently. As I learned from my granddaddy years ago, the relevant phrase is *carpe closum.* That means "seize the close."

This does *not* mean asking for the sale before you have earned the right to do so. Rather, it means working on implementing all that you've learned in Skills One through Fourteen – and *noticing* when your mind has connected with the prospect's in a special way. And then taking action.

Once that happens, you will have encountered what I call the *MasterMind moment* of the sales process: the perfect moment to finalize the commitment ... and *Close and Grow Rich*.

## The Window of Opportunity

Noticing the *MasterMind moment* means noticing when and how the "window of opportunity" opens – not just once, but as a rule, in your sales process.

Noticing the *MasterMind moment* means knowing what the optimum moment for closing typically looks like, sounds like, and feels like in your world.

Noticing the *MasterMind moment* means programming yourself, through continual study and habit, to identify that one critical instant in the sales process when an idea, backed with sufficient emotion, can become illuminated with the spark that lights its transition into tangible reality. You will eventually come to recognize this spark as the culmination of the work you and the prospect have done *together* to harness a massive force that benefits both of you. This force is known by many names, but it is, I believe, the principle that makes all lasting riches possible.

## The MasterMind Principle

Napoleon Hill identified the MasterMind Principle as the phenomenon that occurs when one mind bonds with another in a way that summons greater powers than either mind could summon on its own. When this happens between you and your prospect, the prospect will eventually reach an *emotional peak* as a result of that connection.

When you encounter that emotional peak, rest assured that you have encountered the "defining moment" in your unique sales process.

This MasterMind moment is always the direct result of *your mind working in sync with the other person's on an object of mutual benefit.*

It's the moment when selling becomes easy ... *if* you, the salesperson, take action at the right time. There's a magic moment when there's a very high level of attention, energy, involvement, and rapport, a moment when the other person "gets it."

## Don't Miss the Moment!

Do you know how many sales presentations are delivered every day by "robot" salespeople who insist on talking through all their memorized points, totally oblivious that the peak of interest and emotion from the prospect is coming ... and going?

If you wish to *Close and Grow Rich*, you must *notice* when this moment appears, and you must act on it. Are you one of the elite groups of salespeople who are capable of this? Or are you part of the vast number will stumble into – and out of – the Mastermind moment, and allow the prospect's emotional peak to pass unexploited? (People may do this for any number of startlingly foolish reasons – for instance, the moment may pass because the salesperson is in the middle of a PowerPoint presentation. Who cares what slide you're on? The prospect is ready to buy!)

This critical moment of truth, this MasterMind moment, has nothing to do with the words you memorize ahead of time to say out loud to the other person. It has everything to do with the mind-to-mind *connection* you are able to establish. It has everything to do with the way you see, hear, and experience your relationship with the prospect *before you interact at all*. If you envision yourself and the prospect actually working together, if you envision the prospect benefiting from what you have to offer, then you will be laying the groundwork for this Mastermind moment.

If you lay that groundwork with conscious determination, and resolve to pay more attention to the prospect's emotions than your own, you will be much less likely to miss the moment when it appears!

## The critical principle

Resolve now to benefit from this ancient, undeniable principle:

**Two or more minds, whenever they are fused to a common purpose, harness the power of massive forces indeed.**

Take a close look at the diagram on the next page; return to it once daily for at least the next thirty days, and, each day, study its progression with care.

## Seize the close – Carpe Closum!

The "meet and greet" phase moves to getting information and qualifying. Getting information and qualifying moves to some kind of demonstration. The demonstration moves to a trial close

# The Closing Curve©

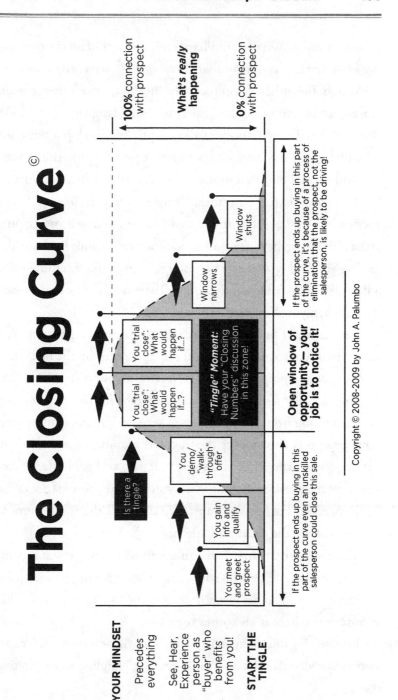

**YOUR MINDSET**

Precedes everything

See, Hear, Experience person as "buyer" who benefits from you!

**START THE TINGLE**

Is there a tingle?

You meet and greet prospect

You gain info and qualify

You demo/ "walk-through" offer

You "trial close": What would happen if...?

You "trial close": What would happen if...?

*"Tingle" Moment:* Have your "Closing Numbers" discussion in this zone!

Window narrows

Window shuts

100% connection with prospect

**What's *really* happening**

0% connection with prospect

If the prospect ends up buying in this part of the curve, it's because of a process of elimination that the prospect, not the salesperson, is likely to be driving!

**Open window of opportunity— your job is to notice it!**

If the prospect ends up buying in this part of the curve even an unskilled salesperson could close this sale.

Copyright © 2008-2009 by John A. Palumbo

of some kind. ("What would happen if ...?") *And all the time you are observing ... looking for that "sweet spot" in the conversation.*

Watch the other person closely, listen to the other person closely, and monitor the other person's body language closely. Do this with persistence, and you will eventually develop a sense for when he or she has hit the very topmost point of emotion, interest, and mental buy-in. Do not miss the peak on that bell curve!

That peak is the customer's "tingle" – the feeling of latent excitement we have all experienced before making a major purchase. That's what you're on the lookout for. Think back on the feeling you had *right before* you bought something exciting – say, a flat-screen TV. That was the tingle! That was the emotional peak! That's when you were ready to buy!

Let me say it once again, because it warrants repetition: You must learn to recognize that peak, the high point on the bell curve *by laying the proper groundwork for it* within your own mind. That requires actually *seeing, hearing, and experiencing* the person using and benefiting from your product or service. You must also watch your prospects closely over the next weeks and months – so you can log some experience and some practice, and get better at recognizing the precise moment when you and the prospect are at the peak together! Finally, you must *take action* at the right moment by envisioning the order and asking for the business.

The peak of that curve is the moment when the person is completely, totally engaged in what you're saying and thinking, the moment when you are *perfectly positioned to close the deal.* **This moment is where it all comes together.**

Recognizing this moment in your world will only come with experience. But identifying it isn't "mind-reading." Finding and exploiting this moment is a *process* you really can master, a process of interacting with your prospects. Once you commit to recognizing this moment, you have truly embarked on the course that leads to Sales Mastery.

## The "tingle"

Salespeople who learn The Closing Curve to watch the sales curve, and "seize the close," really do earn significantly more than salespeople who don't. These are the ones who learn to recognize and seize the opportunity to close when it appears. These are the ones who develop their *empathic intelligence* over time, and use that sense to tell when there really is a "tingle" in the other person.

When that "tingle" is at its strongest, and not a second before or a second after, Sales Masters take action.

In fact, the close can't happen without the "tingle" … and the "tingle" is what makes it possible for us to get the ink of the signature onto the purchase agreement. If the "tingle" phase doesn't happen, the contract won't get signed! You must attend to the one before you expect the other.

Consider a woman who has decided to get married. On the big day, she goes to the altar, stands next to the man of her choice, and says the magic words: "I do." But when did she decide to get married? Long before! So let's say the decision to get married was made six months earlier. All she did was finalize things on the day of the wedding.

In a sales presentation, it's the same thing. The visible "closing" – so-called – should be considered nothing more than the formality. And that's the point I want to leave you with as we come to the conclusion this book. In any "closing" situation, the Sales Master is focused on the "tingle" that makes it possible not to have to ask for the check. The Sales Master knows that the actual *decision* to buy is made well before any salesperson ever gets a signed purchase agreement.

## True story

A Sales Master named Don, who attended one of my seminars a while back, told me the following story.

"I was walking a young couple through a home in a development in central Florida. It was the first time they'd ever bought a home. The husband said, "I love this place. I just don't think any other place we've seen compares with this." The wife nodded and smiled. I could tell that she, too, was thinking about how much she loved the place.

"Whatever they were thinking about, I could tell that the 'tingle' you had mentioned in your seminar was now in the room.

"I now *live* for the moment when the 'tingle' enters the room.

"I knew, because you had reminded me of it so very often during your seminar, that the moment demanded action. Here's what I did. I stood with my hands on my hips. I looked around. And I said, *'You know what? I think this is your home.'*

"The wife just beamed at me, John. A great, big smile. Green light. I checked the husband.

"He smiled and gave a little nod.  It was launch time."

(Pardon the interruption, but did you notice what you just saw? That was the *defining moment* of Don's sale. That's Don's moment of truth. He knows it when it comes along! If he misses it, shame on him! Do you know *your* moment of truth? *And now, back to our story.*)

## Don's Moment of Truth

"I shifted my head, looked down at the floor, looked up at the husband, made eye contact with him, put out my hand, and said, 'It's yours. We'll take care of the paperwork.'

"He thought for just a moment, then grinned, wider than ever, and shook my hand.

"The deal was done. That was it. The closing had just occurred. After all, I was there to facilitate the DECISION, which is a matter of emotion. As you said in your program, the contracts were just a formality. Once we shook hands – they were in.

## Seize it!

Carpe closum! Seize the close! Notice when you are at the peak of the bell curve ... and take action! If you *miss* the top of that bell curve, don't ask for whom the bell tolls ... it tolls for you, because your sale just died!

## You already know how to do this

Believe it! You really do know how to "Seize the Close."

Was there ever a time when you were willing to take action at *precisely the right moment*, and ask the other person to do something that benefited both parties? (For instance: Did you ask your future spouse to marry you? Did you share an idea that sparked a brand new brainstorm – one that both you and the other person loved? Did you turn an acquaintance into a friendship?)

Yes ＿＿＿

No ＿＿＿

Who was it?

＿＿＿＿＿＿＿＿＿＿＿＿＿＿＿＿＿＿＿＿＿＿＿＿＿＿＿＿＿＿

What ultimately happened?

＿＿＿＿＿＿＿＿＿＿＿＿＿＿＿＿＿＿＿＿＿＿＿＿＿＿＿＿＿＿

Before you move on to the epilogue of this book, ponder this question: **When could you tell there was a "tingle" of interest from the other person – and how did you turn that "tingle" into action?**

# PART THREE

Epilogue

# Epilogue

I want to help you revisit and reinforce what you've learned in this book. Please visit

## www.JohnPalumbo.com

so you can access some special content that I've developed for you ... material that will help you "lock in" your reawakened closing skills.

I realize, of course, that the *average* salesperson wouldn't take the time to access these resources ... but there's no doubt about it now. You haven't come this far just to be *good...* you've embarked on this journey so you can become *great.*

I leave you with these wise words:

---

**"Then I asked: 'Does a firm persuasion that a thing is so, make it so?' He replied: 'All Poets believe that it does, and in ages of imagination this firm persuasion removed mountains; but many are not capable of a firm persuasion of anything.'"**

**– William Blake, English poet**

---

Go forth and prosper!

# About the Author

John A. Palumbo is CEO and founder of the Sales DNA Institute, an idea studio and research laboratory for sales and marketing management. Since 1985, he has presented hundreds of dynamic, visionary speeches and seminars internationally on the science of sales and influence. John is a member of the National Speakers Association and brings humor and animation to the platform to help others exceed their sales goals.

John has been instrumental in restructuring the Sales DNA of thousands of individuals from small, family run companies to large scale developers such as Trump Grande International. He has the ability to take individuals and organizations to new dimensions of selling excellence. With more than three decades of selling experience, John has closed over one billion dollars in real estate sales.

He is recipient of The National Association of Home Builders' Sales Manager of the Year Award and The Million Dollar Circle Lifetime Award. He is a prominent member of the Institute of Residential Marketing and has been an instructor for the institute for more than 15 years.

John's other books include *Selling at the Bottom of the Market, The Closing Numbers, What's Your Sales DNA?* and soon to be released, *Salesnosis: The Art of Hypnotic Persuasion.*

## Selling at the Bottom of the Market
A Seven Minute Presentation

How would you like to have a private coaching session with one of the nation's leading sales experts? John's newest book is exactly that. The unique, graphic design takes you from start to finish of precisely what to say *and write* with your next prospective buyer to boost your ability to close more sales ... in even the toughest markets. John has answered the question all sales professionals are asking: "How do we sell to prospects that are afraid of making a buying mistake?" Buyers exist in every market – learn John's simple revelations and ensure that they convert to your sale and not someone else's.

### www.**SellingAtTheBottom**.com

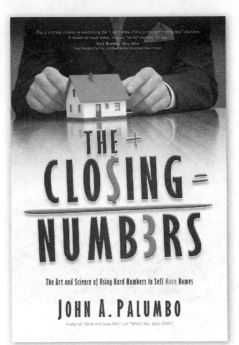

## The Closing Numbers
The Art and Science of Using Hard
Numbers to Sell More Homes

Numbers are the weakest link in the industry. However, when used and explained properly to your prospective home buyer, the numbers can become your strongest selling point. Stop hiding behind excuses about "tough prospects" and "down markets" and exemplify a new way of talking about home ownership that will have your customers asking *you* for the sale. Let's face it – buyers expect you to know the numbers. Luckily enough, John's book makes mastering the numbers a cinch!

## www.**TheClosingNumbers**.com

**What's Your Sales DNA?**
Discover the Hidden Forces that are
Stopping You from Making Millions

As a highly sought after judge for Professional Achievement Awards for over 20 years, John has collected data from all over the country and discovered what sets the *really good* sales agents apart from the *truly great* Sales Masters. *What's Your Sales DNA?* reveals the results of John's research and will cause you to take an introspective look at the hidden forces that are holding you back from making millions.

www.MySalesDNA.com

*Soon to be released*

# Salesnosis
## The Art of Hypnotic Persuasion
By John A. Palumbo

If you are a salesperson, entrepreneur, or business owner set in old, traditional ways of selling, this book may not be for you. However, for the hungry and open-minded, *Salesnosis* offers a powerful and revolutionary approach to capturing a prospect's attention, building credibility, and achieving influence. Turn your next presentation into an irresistible offer with these cutting-edge techniques for any sales situation. Regardless of what you're selling, mastering the art of hypnotic persuasion will create a sudden increase in sales — and dramatically boost your bank account.

www.**Salesnosis**.com